Expanding Work Programs
for Poor Men

Expanding Work Programs
for Poor Men

Lawrence M. Mead

The AEI Press

Publisher for the American Enterprise Institute

WASHINGTON, D.C.

Distributed by arrangement with the Rowman & Littlefield Publishing Group, 4501 Forbes Boulevard, Suite 200, Lanham, Maryland 20706. To order, call toll free 1-800-462-6420 or 1-717-794 3800. For all other inquiries, please contact AEI Press, 1150 Seventeenth Street, N.W., Washington, D.C. 20036, or call 1-800-862-5801.

Library of Congress Cataloging-in-Publication Data

Mead, Lawrence M.
  Expanding work programs for poor men / Lawrence M. Mead.
    p. cm.
  Includes bibliographical references and index.
  ISBN-13: 978-0-8447-4397-4 (cloth)
  ISBN-10: 0-8447-4397-6 (cloth)
  ISBN-13: 978-0-8447-4399-8 (ebook)
  ISBN-10: 0-8447-4399-2 (ebook)
  1. Public welfare—United States. 2. Poor men—Employment—United
States. 3. Poor men—Services for—United States. 4. Manpower
policy—United States. I. Title.
  HV95.M346 2010
  362.5'840973—dc22

Printed in the United States of America

Contents

Acknowledgments

My thanks to the many people and institutions that made this study possible. Funding came in part from New York University, which financed a sabbatical leave, and from the National Research Initiative at the American Enterprise Institute (AEI), where I was a visiting scholar during 2008 and 2009. At AEI, Jon Flugstad was a very capable research assistant. He helped organize the two conferences that I held in connection with the project, and he is chiefly responsible for the state survey of men's work programs that I report in chapter 6.

My thanks also to Isabel Sawhill and Ron Haskins of the Brookings Institution, who commissioned my initial paper on the men's work problem. Among the many who helped with ideas or contacts in the states, I especially credit Elaine Sorensen of the Urban Institute and Myles Schlank of the U.S. Office of Child Support Enforcement (OCSE). I also credit the many research organizations whose findings I draw on, especially the Manpower Demonstration Research Corporation (MDRC). Without their work, my project would have been impossible.

I also thank those who gave me comments and reactions during several presentations on the project at AEI and OCSE and at several academic conferences. The manuscript was reviewed by Robert Lerman, Ronald Mincy, Elaine Sorensen, and two anonymous reviewers commissioned by AEI. Their suggestions definitely improved the product, but I did not adopt all of them, and responsibility for the final product remains mine.

Finally, I thank the many state and local officials who took the time to talk to me during my interviews in six states. More than I realized, they are already well down the road toward developing better work programs for poor men. A great deal of what I report here is gleaned from them.

List of Tables

Commonly Used Acronyms

AFDC	Aid to Families with Dependent Children
CEO	Center for Employment Opportunities
CSE	Child Support Enforcement (state and local)
EITC	Earned Income Tax Credit
MDRC	Manpower Demonstration Research Corporation
MPRI	Michigan Prison Reentry Initiative
NCP Choices	Non-Custodial Parent Choices (Texas)
NEWWS	National Evaluation of Welfare to Work Strategies
OAG	Office of the Attorney General (Texas)
OCSE	Office of Child Support Enforcement (federal)
PFS	Parents' Fair Share
PRWORA	Personal Responsibility and Work Opportunity Reconciliation Act of 1996
RIO	Reintegration of Offenders (Texas)
TANF	Temporary Assistance for Needy Families
TJRD	Transitional Jobs Reentry Demonstration
TWC	Texas Workforce Commission
WIA	Workforce Investment Act (workforce system)

Introduction

Even amid the current economic recovery, America's struggle to overcome poverty continues. On both right and left, Americans and their leaders do not accept that large numbers of people should be needy in one of the richest countries on earth. Republicans and Democrats differ about much, but both parties show a serious commitment to overcoming the poverty problem.

The most recent watershed in that struggle was welfare reform. In the 1990s, through a largely bipartisan effort, family welfare was transformed to require that most welfare mothers work in return for aid. Coupled with new benefits and superb economic conditions, those requirements reduced the welfare rolls by well over half. Work levels among poor mothers rose dramatically while family poverty fell, albeit less sharply.

Now attention is being paid to nonworking men, because their employment is also crucial to uplifting families. How to get them to work more steadily is my subject here. Much of my approach is modeled on welfare reform. Poor fathers, like poor mothers, need both help and hassle. That is, they need more help from government than they are getting. But they must also be expected to help themselves. We need to demand work—and, if necessary, to enforce it.

This study is the first to ask what a serious effort to raise poor men's work levels would mean. I ask, in effect, how can we achieve welfare reform for men? The parallel to the earlier reform cannot be exact because most nonworking men are not on welfare or receiving any government benefit. We must seek other points of leverage. It turns out that government is already much involved with many of the men who concern us. It demands that absent fathers pay child support, and it expects ex-offenders leaving the prisons to work as a condition of parole. The immediate goals are to obtain income for families and to forestall convicts returning to crime. But these

1

requirements could also be a basis for requiring men to work and thus raising their work levels. The germ of a male work test already exists in the institutions we have.

In this book, I look first at the scale of the men's work problem and what seems to be its causes. That requires an excursion into the psychology of male nonwork, which has seldom been explored. I go on to examine experimental programs in which a serious attempt was made to get more poor men working. Such programs appear able to raise work levels—if well implemented.

Could such programs be implemented widely? My own research concentrates especially on this question. A surprising number of states have already instituted programs like this, even though Washington has been little aware of it. My own interviews in several states uncovered the reasons why some states innovate in this area and some do not. The more enterprising states suggest that, as in welfare reform, the real solution to poverty is institutional—building new programs that can both promote and require work for needy adults.

Finally, I draw conclusions for national policy. I recommend a best form for poor men's work programs. I advise cautious expansion of these programs and additional evaluations to learn more about them. I also recommend higher wage subsidies for low-paid workers. As in welfare reform, linking benefits and requirements is the way forward.

Poverty and Work

If nothing else, welfare reform confirmed that employment is central to overcoming poverty. When families are poor in America, the immediate reason is usually that parents do not work consistently. Accordingly, raising employment among poor adults has been a central goal of social policy ever since poverty first became a national issue in the 1960s. Even programs seemingly aimed at other things—such as improving education or child care—have among their goals getting more poor fathers and mothers to work more regularly.

The poor work much less than the nonpoor. Table I-1 shows that, in general, work levels in the American adult population run high. Nearly two-thirds of persons aged sixteen and over worked at some time in 2009, and

TABLE I-1

EMPLOYMENT RATE BY POVERTY STATUS OF PERSONS AGED SIXTEEN
AND OVER AND FAMILY HEADS, 2009 (PERCENT)

	Persons	Men	Women	All family heads	Female heads	With children under 18 — All family heads	With children under 18 — Female heads
All income levels							
Worked at any time	65	71	60	70	67	80	73
Full time/full year	42	48	35	49	42	56	45
Did not work	35	29	40	30	33	20	27
Income below poverty							
Worked at any time	36	41	32	46	48	53	52
Full time/full year	9	12	7	15	13	17	14
Did not work	64	59	68	54	52	47	48

NOTE: Full time means at least thirty-five hours per week; full year means at least fifty weeks per year.
SOURCE: U.S. Census Bureau, *March 2010 Annual Social and Economic Supplement,* tables 14, 15, 22.

42 percent worked full time and full year. Yet among adults under the poverty line, only 36 percent worked at all. Only 9 percent worked full year and full time—less than a quarter of the population rate. If we contrasted poor with nonpoor, the differences would be even greater. Similar gaps prevail if we look at men, women, heads of family, or female family heads. In the population, 80 percent of family heads with children worked in 2009, with 56 percent full time and full year, but among the poor, work rates ran dramatically lower, especially full time and full year. These figures are for a recession year. In better times, work levels for both the population and the poor would be slightly higher, but the gap would remain.

The point is not that people are first poor and then decline to work. Rather, they are poor largely *because* they lack work. Nonemployment is usually the principal cause of working-age poverty. It is not the only cause—many other factors mediate that link between employment and poverty, particularly wage levels and family size. There are working poor—people who work regular hours yet are poor, usually due to either low wages or large families where no other family members work.

However, the working poor are far outnumbered by the nonworking poor. The link between nonwork and poverty is extraordinarily potent. Whatever the precise connection is, poverty—especially serious and sustained poverty—is deeply involved with low work levels. It is difficult to imagine overcoming family poverty without poor adults working more consistently. Raising their work levels has more impact than anything else.

Reasoning like this lay behind welfare reform, which aimed above all to raise work levels among poor single mothers, many of whom are needy for lack of jobs. Aid to Families with Dependent Children (AFDC), the principal cash welfare program, had long supported needy female-headed families without a serious work expectation. That was the main reason it was unpopular. Work programs attached to AFDC to which welfare mothers might be assigned were first seriously expanded in the Family Support Act of 1988. Then, in 1996, the Personal Responsibility and Work Opportunity Reconciliation Act (PRWORA) replaced AFDC with Temporary Assistance for Needy Families. TANF mandated that states move half of recipients into work activities by 2002, on pain of cuts in their federal funding.

Work levels rose sharply—on and off the rolls. In 1993, only 44 percent of poor mothers with children worked at all, with only 9 percent full time and full year. By 1999, those numbers had jumped to 64 and 17 percent, respectively.[1] TANF's new work requirements were the main impetus behind this change, although a superb economy and new wage and child care subsidies also contributed.[2] Although some of the work gain was lost in the ensuing recessions, employment levels for poor mothers have remained substantially higher than before welfare reform. That shift was the main cause of the drop in the caseload of around 70 percent that occurred between 1994 and 2008. Even in the recent recession, TANF cases went back up only slightly.

However, if poor mothers were working more, poor fathers were working less. Even unusually low unemployment and growing real wages in the 1990s raised their work levels only slightly. As Table I-1 shows, in 2009, only 41 percent of poor men worked at all, only 12 percent full time and full year, compared with figures of 71 and 48 percent, respectively, for the population as a whole. Those levels were below those for poor female family heads with children, even though mothers usually have to arrange child care in order to work.

Men have received more attention recently chiefly because of a wave of men returning from prison following rising incarceration in recent decades. A movement has arisen to help ex-offenders and other poor men move into employment and thus reintegrate in society.

Misconceptions

For that quest to succeed, government must avoid past errors. Welfare reform was delayed for decades because the contention about it was unduly *partisan*. In the 1960s and 1970s, the debate focused mostly on how much government should do for the poor, with Democrats and liberals typically asking for more and Republicans and conservatives for less. The debate also focused on *opportunity* as the answer to poverty or dependency. Roughly, those left of center wanted government to emancipate the poor from perceived impediments to working, whereas the right counted on the private market to do so. Finally, the discourse was *economistic*, focused chiefly on the benefits welfare provided and the incentives those benefits generated for or against marriage and employment. Although some welfare reform plans tried to promote employment, they conceived of it more as another benefit to be provided to the recipients than as an obligation incumbent upon them.

In the 1980s and 1990s, a more mature debate emerged. PRWORA was in some ways highly partisan, the doing largely of Republicans, but it embodied changes in work and child support requirements that reflected experience. Evaluations suggested that the Family Support Act of 1988 had been too cautious in enforcing work. It had put too many clients in education and training, whereas going to work in available jobs generated more gains in employment and earnings. Accordingly, PRWORA required more welfare mothers to enter work activities, and it shifted these activities toward "work first"—entering available jobs rather than training.

The discourse also focused less on expanding opportunity for the poor than on obligating them to fulfill their responsibilities, both to work and to pay child support. Reform was also seen less in economic and more in institutional terms. The main lever for change was no longer incentives but the expanded work and child support requirements that states were to implement on the ground, that is, at the local level, where recipients were served. Although such benefits as child care and wage subsidies still played a role, economics ceded to statecraft as the chief language of policy.[3]

The emerging men's debate will have to undergo a similar shift to be fruitful. In Congress, liberals have responded to the men's problem chiefly by throwing money at it. Conservatives seek instead to engage faith-based organizations to serve the men. The first approach would build up government in a conventional sense, whereas the second would restrict it. Politicians also tend to treat the men as unfortunates who bear no responsibility for their condition. The press depicts them as oppressed by external conditions—as child support defaulters overwhelmed by their arrears or as ex-offenders without support in the community.[4] As in welfare, policy thinking is economic, framed in terms of new services and incentives.

As before, solutions require that policymakers focus on solving the problem, not on partisan combat; they must be prepared to enforce work as well as facilitate it; and they must think in institutional more than in economic terms. The way forward is to graft new work programs onto the child support and criminal justice systems that already deal with low-income men. Only in this way can nonworking men, like welfare mothers, get both the help and hassle they need to work more.

A Look Ahead

In the chapters that follow, I first provide more detail about the men's work problem. Failure to work regularly is the largest single problem poor men have, although it is far from the only one. The two key groups of men who often have work problems are those failing to pay child support and those emerging from prison on parole (chapter 1). The causes of nonwork include both economic and cultural conditions. As with welfare mothers, the key to getting more men to work lies in some combination of new benefits and work requirements (chapter 2).

Some promising work programs have already appeared in both child support (chapter 3) and criminal justice (chapter 4). In both areas we see the development of new institutions to deal with growing family abandonment and crime. In both areas, mere enforcement has proved insufficient.

The new programs seek to promote work and other good outcomes through new services as well as requirements. Evaluations suggest that they are promising.

Implementing such programs, however, poses substantial challenges (chapter 5). Nonetheless, a survey of the states shows that half or more have already developed work programs aimed at these men, even with little federal support (chapter 6). Field research in six states clarified the political and administrative factors that determine how aggressively states pursue these programs (chapter 7).

In light of all the evidence, I recommend a form of work program that would be mandatory and work focused. Ideally, enhanced work enforcement would be coupled with improved work subsidies for low-income men who worked steadily and paid their child support (chapter 8). It is too soon to mandate work programs on the states, but Washington should support their cautious expansion, chiefly through better funding and more evaluation (chapter 9).

1

Poor Men's Work Problems

This chapter describes the men's work problem in more depth. Lack of steady employment is the most serious problem poor men have, although far from the only one. Getting them to work more is the best thing society can do for them.

Poor Men and Work

Men aged sixteen to fifty are those most expected to work, although for teenagers the first obligation would be to finish school. In 2009, 9.1 million men in this age range were poor, or 12 percent of the total. Of these poor men, 71 percent were white, but Hispanics (30 percent) and blacks (20 percent) were overrepresented relative to their shares of the population.[1]

Table 1-1 shows the percentages of poor and nonpoor men in this age range who worked full time and full year or, alternatively, did not work at all in 2009, and the figures are broken out by age and race or ethnic group. Among the nonpoor, nearly three-fifths worked full time and full year. This was a recession year—in better times, work levels would run higher. Employment also rises dramatically from ages sixteen to twenty-four to later ages, as men get fully into their careers. The story is similar for all racial and ethnic groups, although blacks and Native Americans show somewhat lower work levels than average.

For poor men, the story is very different. Here only 13 percent report working full time and full year, and more than half did not work at all during the year. Again, work levels would be higher in better times. Employment fails to rise much from the younger ages to the older. Poor youths often fail to make a successful transition to adulthood. Somehow they do not, like better-off men, mature into regular, reliable workers. Already by the age of fifty, most of these men have left the labor force.

TABLE 1-1

MEN WORKING FULL TIME/FULL YEAR AND NOT WORKING,
BY AGE, RACE, AND POVERTY LEVEL, 2009 (PERCENT)

	Ages							
	16–50		16–24		25–35		36–50	
	FT/ FY	No work	FT/ FY	No work	FT/ FY	No work	FT/ FY	No work
Above Poverty								
Total	59	16	21	40	68	8	74	8
White	60	14	23	37	69	7	75	7
Black	51	26	15	53	59	17	68	15
Native American	50	25	20	52	64	9	66	13
Asian	65	16	19	53	72	9	80	6
Hispanic	57	17	27	41	65	8	69	9
Below Poverty								
Total	13	52	6	63	17	40	17	52
White	15	47	7	58	20	34	19	48
Black	7	69	3	78	10	58	9	67
Native American	7	63	0	70	14	48	8	69
Asian	12	57	4	63	11	59	24	49
Hispanic	20	40	7	60	26	27	26	35

NOTE: The category of working but less than full time/full year is omitted. Racial categories do not overlap. Native American includes American Indian and Alaska Native. Racial groups add to less than total because Native Hawaiians and Other Pacific Islanders and persons of two or more races are omitted. Hispanics are an ethnic category and may be of any race.
SOURCE: Author's tabulations from U.S. Census Bureau, *Current Population Survey*, March 2010.

Of course, as mentioned above, the link between poverty and nonwork is to a great extent definitional. The poor are necessarily those without work. Nonwork is poverty by another name. Yet the association is far from perfect, and group differences are revealing. Hispanics have the highest work levels, confirming their image as "working poor." This partly reflects the status of many as recent immigrants, often illegal. Blacks have the lowest work rates, particularly among young men, among whom 78 percent report no employment at all.

Over time, the men's problem has been getting worse, not better. Since at least 1979, rates of labor-force participation (that is, rates of working or seeking work) have been falling for younger men with no more than a high school education. Those rates stabilized for white and Hispanic men in the 1990s, but they continued to fall for blacks—despite the unusually good wages and job prospects of that decade. Rates of actual employment improved slightly for all groups in the 1990s, but blacks' work rates still lagged around twenty points below those of the other groups. And these figures understate black joblessness because they exclude the many black men incarcerated for crime.[2]

Regular employment has ceased to be usual for many low-skilled men. These men typically work erratically and, when not working, subsist on a combination of support from families, the few public benefits they may receive, and illegal employment, such as the drug trade. This change has devastated low-income areas, depriving families not only of income, but also of functioning fathers who can set an example for their children.[3]

Fatherless children tend to drop out of school more often and get involved in unwed pregnancy or crime at a young age, thus continuing the pattern. The lack of reliable fathers in the ghetto is like a wound from which families never fully recover. "Like plants bending toward a distant sun," Jason DeParle has written, children still orient to the absent father, even if he is far away in prison.[4] It is tempting to write such men off, yet in fact they are indispensable. No recovery for the inner city is imaginable unless these men once again come to constitute a *working* class.

Nonwork and Other Problems

The most immediate result of male nonwork is that men themselves are poor, always scrambling to make ends meet. And from that many other social problems follow. The most obvious is family abandonment. Mothers refuse to marry men who are not reliable providers, even if the women have children with them. After a history of nonsupport, they will likely drive the men out of the house.[5] Failure as breadwinners is thus one of the principal causes of unwed pregnancy, which has overtaken low-income America since the 1960s. In 1965, the "Moynihan Report" expressed alarm that a quarter of black children were born out of wedlock, but that rate has since soared to 70 percent for blacks, compared to 50 percent for Hispanics and 33 percent for whites.[6]

Men who do not work regularly are more often involved in crime, especially drug selling, as a substitute or supplement for regular jobs. That in turn entails high risks of addiction, violence, conviction, and incarceration. The rate of violent crime soared from 161 offenses per 100,000 population in 1960 to 758 in 1991, before declining to 467 in 2007. The comparable rates for property crime were 1,726, 5,140, and 3,264, respectively. In response, the rate of imprisonment also soared, so that in 2008, 2.3 million Americans were behind bars, in federal or state prison or in local jails.[7] Perhaps 13 million Americans have a felony conviction—7 percent of the population and 12 percent of males. Probably 3 million are former prisoners.[8]

Some believe that the problems apparently caused by nonwork are really due to other forces. Mothers may reject their partners over nonwork, but they are even more likely to do so over the men's domestic violence, infidelity, or involvement in crime or drugs.[9] Rather than nonwork causing the family problem, perhaps the family problem is the real source of nonwork and other male dysfunctions. Similarly, crime may be due not to nonwork but to "criminogenic" attitudes that dispose men to break the law. They must give up crime as a way of life before they are even receptive to working regularly.

Despite this complexity, it is clear that higher work levels promote better outcomes for both parents and children, even if we cannot specify all the causal connections. Regular employment does make men more marriageable, and whether ex-offenders work is a major determinant of whether they avoid recidivism, even if other factors are involved. Getting a good job does help ex-offenders—especially older men—turn away from crime.[10] Whatever men's other problems are, work will ameliorate them. For men, steady work is a crucial passport to a meaningful life.

Work as Strategic

Another argument for a work focus is that it offers more leverage over men's problems in the short run than other approaches society might take. The deepest difficulties for disadvantaged men probably do lie in crime and family life. Nonworking men are disproportionately black and Hispanic, and these two minorities also dominate serious crime. Blacks and Hispanics comprised 13 and 16 percent, respectively, of the national population in 2008, but they accounted for 40 and 20 percent, respectively, of men behind bars in that year. Whites comprised 80 percent of the population but only 34 percent of the inmates.[11] As many as 30 percent of young black men today may have a criminal record.[12] And as mentioned earlier, the breakup and nonformation of families is most serious among minorities. Among blacks and many Hispanics, the expectation now is that children will grow up without fathers.

But government has so far found few answers to crime and unwed pregnancy. The prison reentry movement offers some hope to reduce recidivism, as discussed in chapter 4, and the U.S. Administration for Children and Families is working on programs to strengthen marriage. But major progress on these fronts is still distant. By comparison, raising work levels is something government knows how to do. Welfare reform showed that it could be achieved through a combination of work enforcement and new benefits. Government has solved many of the practical problems involved in work promotion, including how to motivate staffs and clients and how to hold programs accountable. What worked for welfare mothers can, at least in principle, work for nonworking men as well.

Politics argues the same way. The public regrets the decline of the family but is unready to stigmatize single mothers.[13] The black community is unready to accept the direct promotion of marriage as a solution to poverty. Better to raise men's work levels and child support payments as first steps, and improved relations with spouses and children should follow.[14] Although locking up criminals has recently been popular, it has reached a limit, as chapter 4 shows. In contrast, promoting work for poor adults is extremely popular. Working confers membership in society as nothing else does. Nonworkers themselves typically accept a work obligation, at least in principle, and the public is ready to spend to achieve it, as welfare reform demonstrated.[15]

Men's problems might call for a variety of services, but a work focus is comprehensible to the public and supportable where a more complex strategy is not. As welfare reform showed, in the name of work, our leaders can change the bureaucracy and fund many services besides just job placement. The work mission has an organizing force that nothing else does.

Key Groups

There are 9 million working-aged poor men, but the groups where government has the most leverage are much smaller. One is child support defaulters—men who already owe child support to former families but who fail to pay it due to employment problems. In 2007, the most recent data, an estimated 714,000 noncustodial fathers owed child support to poor mothers but paid either none or less than was due.[16] Presumably most of these men were themselves poor or low income. Most likely, their failure to pay had some connection to employment problems.

The other key group is ex-offenders exiting the prisons on parole. In 2007, 721,161 ex-offenders left federal and state prisons, and 821,177 were on parole in that year. As these numbers imply, parole is usually short term, with 67 percent of cases leaving parole in 2007.[17] In most states parolees are obligated to work as a condition of parole. Sketchy information suggests that although most parolees find jobs quickly on leaving prison, they have trouble maintaining employment, and their work rates fall over time.[18] A rough estimate is that 60 percent of parolees—492,706—have significant problems working.[19]

These two groups comprised 1.2 million men in 2007 who were already supposed to be working, yet had difficulty doing so. That total is somewhat overstated because the two populations overlap—at least 70 percent of male ex-offenders are also noncustodial fathers.[20] This makes the cost estimates I offer below conservative, as the actual need may be smaller than 1.2 million.

I do not directly address here how best to help the much larger numbers of poor men who also have employment problems but currently face no obligation to work. Not all poor men are fathers, and only a minority are ex-offenders. Many, however, are likely to become absent fathers or offenders at some point. The groups I have defined are probably the most disadvantaged of poor men. These are the men whose nonwork poses the greatest difficulty for themselves, their families, and society. They are also the men who have proved hardest to help. Getting them to work, if it can be done, would pay the largest benefits in terms of reducing poverty and other social problems.

2

Causes of Nonwork

To solve the work problem we must first identify its causes.[1] Those forces become levers that policymakers might seize to change behavior. Assuming jobs are available, what can explain why men fail to work regularly when they obviously need income? That behavior appears irrational, so the psychology behind nonwork cannot be straightforward. We need to delve more deeply into poor men's motivation than social policymakers have done.

Approaches to Nonwork

Social scientists give two conflicting accounts of male nonwork. Economists typically assume that it reflects economizing; that is, men are acting rationally so as to maximize their utilities. If they are working less than they once did, that must be because work has become less worthwhile or available than before. The other, cultural approach views the same behavior as dysfunctional; that is, nonworking men are expressing desires but violating their own interests and values—and those of their families and society as well. This behavior is driven by a demand for decent treatment on the job and a drive for respect that are particularly strong in men.

The Economic Approach. Economists assume that men will work if working is worth more to them than not working. Therefore, employment should vary directly with wages. If men are paid more for working, more non-workers will take jobs; if they are paid less, fewer will do so. This is called the substitution effect. And indeed, as wages among low-skilled men (those with a high school education or less) stagnated or fell during the 1970s and 1980s, the work level of this group also fell. On this logic, economists commonly infer that the falling wages directly caused falling employment.

14

However, lower wages also generate an incentive to work more. When pay per hour falls, men already working must put in more hours to cover their financial needs. Conversely, higher wages allow workers to cover these needs with fewer hours. On this logic, employment should vary inversely with wages—as wages go down, work levels should go up. This is called the income effect. When wages change over time, whether the substitution or income effect will dominate is unclear a priori. Work levels might go up or down.

Several economists estimate that, at least for low-paid workers, the substitution effect dominates. Therefore, lower wages have driven work levels down. However, these estimates rest on data before 1990.[2] During the 1990s, real wages for the low skilled rose, especially late in the decade. Work levels for poor single mothers also rose sharply, as is consistent with the economic theory, although welfare reform and the new benefits also helped. For low-skilled men, however, the work increase was tepid, and for low-skilled black men labor-force participation rates continued to fall even during the 1990s. That is inconsistent with the theory. So is the fact that low-skilled black men work at much lower levels than other low-skilled men. Some force other than lower pay must be driving their work levels down.[3]

Some economists also argue that, for disadvantaged men, jobs not only pay less but have become less available. Employers, they believe, have become less patient with low-skilled workers than formerly. Pay now varies far more according to a worker's education than it once did, leaving the low skilled worse off. Under pressure from restructuring and globalization, employers demand that low-paid employees show adaptability and produce without problems or be replaced.[4] But this argument cannot explain why millions of unskilled immigrants from Latin America and Asia are now at work in the U.S. economy. Nor can it account for the large variations in work levels among different groups of poor men, as shown in table 1-1.

Yet another hypothesis is that native-born blacks have become less employable than other low-skilled groups. Economists once thought that the flood of women into the labor force during the 1970s and 1980s drove down wages and employment for young blacks, but during the 1990s there is no evidence of this.[5] George Borjas argues that rapid immigration from Mexico, both legal and illegal, has depressed unskilled male wages and employment. Anecdotal evidence suggests that employers often do spurn native-born blacks in favor of women or illegal aliens, viewing them as more tractable. But other economists question these effects. They are, in any event, too small to explain the very low black male work levels or their failure to rise more in the hot labor market of the 1990s.[6]

One fact that used to make male nonwork seem rational is that drugs and other illicit trades seemed to offer better opportunities to the low-skilled male than legal but low-paid jobs. Some view poor men's involvement in drugs as a direct response to their inability to get legitimate employment.[7] However, returns to drug selling have fallen since the 1980s. Most drug gang members today make barely more than they would in legal employment, while they also face high risks of violence and arrest. Most of the returns go to the gang leaders. Drug dealing no longer seems a rational alternative to legal but low-paid jobs.[8]

Other barriers may appear to block employment for the poor. The mismatch theory asserts that jobs have become less accessible to the inner-city poor, either because openings have shifted from the cities to the suburbs or overseas or because the urban jobs still available now demand more education and skills than poor adults have.[9] This theory, too, seemed more plausible during the 1970s and 1980s, when deindustrialization raged, than it did during the 1990s, when legions of unskilled immigrants as well as welfare mothers found jobs in cities. Even in a globalizing economy, most jobs do not demand a four-year college education, and many of these jobs still pay well.[10]

The Cultural Approach. The cultural interpretation is that nonworking men fail to take advantage even of the jobs they can get. In this view, the apparent association of lower wages with lower employment is spurious. Neither directly causes the other. Rather, both result from a breakdown in work discipline, which is the real driver. Low-income men, particularly blacks, have become less reliable employees. As a result, they are paid less, *and* they also work less, because they are often fired or drop out of jobs. This logic is consistent with employers' loss of patience with low-skilled workers. One argument against the cultural view is that schooling levels for men— our best measure of labor quality—continue to improve, although educational standards have no doubt fallen compared to decades ago.[11]

Since the 1990s, many low-skilled men may seem deterred from working because of wage deductions to pay child support or because they are incarcerated. In the 1990s, these factors likely overwhelmed the greater disposition to work that higher wages might have caused.[12] Wage deductions and imprisonment could be viewed as disincentives or barriers to work, consistent with the economic approach. But the behavior that generates these sanctions is not optimizing, but self-defeating, consistent with the cultural viewpoint.

The best evidence for the cultural theory comes from ethnographic accounts of the attitudes and behavior of nonworking men. If disincentives such as low wages explained nonwork, we would find these men complaining about low wages and demanding to be paid more, in the practical style of trade unionists who bargain with bosses over working conditions. Ethnographers find, however, that the main reason the men do not work is not calculations of advantage but the confusions of private life. Immersed in conflicts with spouses and other personal struggles, they are not organized well enough to work, whatever the wage. So although they affirm working in principle, they fail to follow through on their own intentions.[13]

The culture of nonwork resembles the culture of poverty in general. Poor adults are seldom rebels or bohemians. They do not reject conventional values, such as the work ethic or marital fidelity. Yet commonly they fail to achieve them. The gap between norms and actual behavior is much wider than it usually is for the better off. Differences in outward opportunities are insufficient to explain this.[14] More important, the men often yield to the temptations of the street, such as the drug trade, rather than going straight.[15]

A more pessimistic interpretation is that the most alienated men have abandoned traditional values entirely, in favor of a life that defiantly seeks power and pleasure on the street.[16] But this view cannot account for the air of disappointment and depression that hangs over lower-class society. The culture of poverty is, above all, a culture of defeat.[17] If poor men really rejected conventional values, they would challenge society more than they do. When faced by some new demand by the authorities, their usual response is not aggressive but passive aggressive. Most neither comply nor protest, but withdraw. This reflects their conviction that they are losers and mainstream society has no place for them.[18] That instinct explains the low turnout in men's programs even when the benefits offered are generous and undemanding, as I note below. The work problem cannot be solved without overcoming this profound estrangement from society.

Male Demands. All this applies to poor adults in general. But the problem of male nonwork appears to involve additional dimensions that derive from male psychology. The following account is somewhat speculative, but it draws on the ethnographic accounts already mentioned. Most of this research is about blacks, but there is no reason to think that the psychology of male nonwork differs importantly by race or ethnicity. Disadvantaged Hispanic youth show the same self-defeating patterns as poor blacks, as do the long-term white poor of Appalachia.[19] The psychology of male defeat is universal.

Welfare reform revealed that poor mothers are surprisingly accepting of employment. Many had worked off the books while drawing aid. For many women, being required to work on the books was not a major change. The usual barriers were the logistics of arranging child care and, often, a lack of confidence. Hence the evolution of welfare policy toward work programs that are both demanding and supportive. They not only require welfare women to work but also help them achieve it.[20]

Nonworking men, typically, are more demanding. That is because work is usually *more* important to them, not less. Poor mothers tend to take the wage they are offered. Black male youth, in contrast, typically demand higher wages before they will work than do comparable white youth. Economists say that they have a higher "reservation wage."[21] But this framing again suggests a quality of calm calculation that is lacking. This is not optimizing behavior in the usual, monetary sense. Young black men will often refuse to work for "chump change" even if it means not working at all. Or they accept jobs but then find them unrewarding or abusive, so they leave in a huff or are fired. They are defending their self-esteem rather than maximizing their income.[22]

Low-skilled youth feel that employers treat them as expendable, firing them on the least provocation. To the employers, however, it seems that the men simply don't want to work. So bosses grow wary of hiring them, particularly minorities and ex-offenders. One cannot call such preferences racist in the usual sense of a generalized hostility to blacks because black employers voice the same complaints as whites.[23] Economists may say the men behave "as if" they do not find work worth their time. Again, that implies a capacity to decide rationally. Actually, the men violate their own intentions, which are to work and get ahead.

Successful men keep assertiveness in line. That usually reflects early conditioning. Middle-class boys of all races internalize the values and lifestyles of their parents. Obeying their elders—especially their fathers—prepares them later to obey their teachers and employers. Even in the ghetto, fathers in two-parent families school their sons to be reliable family men.[24] To be sure, working does not solve all their problems. They still have to struggle for adequate wages, through earning raises or promotions or through trade union or political action. But by becoming steady workers, they at least get a foot on the ladder. That is the formation that nonworking men and youth typically lack.

The Quest for Respect. At the heart of nonwork is not economic behavior but men's hunger for "dignity" or "respect." More than most women, men at all income levels typically work not just to make money but to "be somebody." Gaining respect means that others recognize your importance and grant you a place in the world. The male quest is to get out front for some cause and by so doing to vindicate oneself. That drive motivates men's achievements, but it is dangerous unless it is harnessed to being employed and supporting families.[25] One key to poverty is that the quest for respect has lost those moorings in low-income areas.

Poor men feel the same drive as better-off men, but they are less able to satisfy it. Typically, they grow up in weak families and disordered neighborhoods where, during their formative years, they do not learn the behaviors needed for advancement. Most families are female-headed. The mothers seek to socialize their sons but do it less well than a two-parent family could do. The child is thus not ready for school and tends to do poorly there and later on the job. Each rejection makes the quest for dignity more desperate, producing rebellion, which produces further rejection, in a descending spiral. In the middle class, by contrast, boys of all races learn early to satisfy their parents, then their teachers and bosses, in an ascending spiral.

Paradoxically, the social problems of nonworking men arise initially from virtue rather than vice—the search for a meaningful life. To observers, the men seem out of control and threatening, yet they themselves feel pow-erless to be anybody.[26] Unable to make any impact on the world, many unskilled youth turn away from the legitimate roles of worker and family man. They develop an oppositional street culture where prestige is won by physical toughness rather than by conventional achievement. Many go into the drug trade as a way to vindicate themselves against the disapproval of society. Unfortunately, to pursue recognition this way proves destructive for both them and their communities.[27]

They also usually fail to form their own families. They father children but then abandon them and the mothers because the demands of marriage and fatherhood are too great.[28] An economic logic is too narrow to capture the dynamics. Low-income men might seem to be deterred from working when their wages are garnished to pay child support. This reduces the effec-tive wage they can earn, so they calculate that working is no longer worth-while. Firsthand accounts, however, suggest that the men are much more blocked by the humiliation and anger they feel at the child support system and, often, the mother who turned them in. Child support is not just a cost but the badge of their failure as husbands and fathers.[29]

This perspective helps to explain one of the mysteries of poverty—why poor men on average are less employable than poor women, even though the latter have children to deal with. The reason may be that their lot in life is less affirming. Poor women find their identity chiefly as mothers. They typi-cally believe they can succeed in that role, even if outside observers demur. They have to meet community standards for their children, but they are not in direct competition with other mothers. They also have had their own mothers as role models, even if their fathers were absent.[30] For them, work-ing is secondary. It usually poses practical problems, not a crisis of identity.

Men, by contrast, are wired to achieve self-esteem chiefly through efforts outside the home. That forces them into the labor market, a far more com-petitive arena than motherhood. They have bought into the success ethos of the wider society, and, following the civil rights reforms, they can no longer blame failure on systematic injustice.[31] But they are up against other men much better prepared than themselves. They often lack fathers to guide them, and government does little to help them. So their failure to compete is all but inevitable. Hence their prickly defensiveness, which often blocks them from working at all, to their own cost.

Work before Family. One implication of this analysis is that, for men, work must come before family. Men themselves think this. They seek work first and foremost to vindicate themselves. Getting money to support families or other ends is also important, but does not cut as deep. Even a man of independent means, who need not work, will feel unfulfilled unless he is accomplishing something that people recognize in the outside world. Many educated women feel the same, but for low-income women, work is typically more instrumental, something they often do mostly for income.

In appraising men, women also put work before marriage. They demand to see that a man is a reliable provider before they will contemplate marriage with him. Many poor men fail to provide; they often get into drugs, crime, and spousal abuse as well. They seldom justify themselves. They do not argue coolly that available jobs are not worthwhile; they simply behave badly in ways that even they cannot explain. So the women give up on them and raise their children alone.[32] So for men, success at work becomes the passport to marriage and family life. Without steady work, a man may father children, but he cannot become a daddy in the conventional sense.[33]

Some studies suggest the reverse—that marriage can be the key to employment. The married man is likely to work harder than the unmarried to support his children. In various ways, his wife may also help him succeed on the job. So if society could promote more stable marriages among poor partners, that might help solve the work problem.[34] Nevertheless, although marriage and work are strongly associated, a causal link is less clear: rather than either work or marriage causing the other, both reflect the competences a man must have either to work or to marry.[35] Ethnographic accounts favor the view that work is primary. We read that whether men are reliable providers shapes whether they marry. The same observers do not suggest that whether men marry determines whether they work.[36]

If work is primary, then one implication is that men must prove themselves first of all in competition with other workers. In legitimate employment, workers focus on the job, and whether a man succeeds with women outside the workplace is irrelevant. Indeed, as feminists often complain, American bosses typically make few allowances for whether a worker has a family or not. It is true that street youth can impress their friends by "scoring" with women and fathering children out of wedlock. But these rewards are a poor substitute for the more solid rewards that come from succeeding in legal jobs and then in marriage, and street men know it.

This appraisal also implies, since most workers are men, that men must prove themselves centrally with other men, and only then with women. Marginalized men spend much of their time in the neighborhood, not at the workplace.[37] They interact with women, and their troubled relations with the opposite sex are highly visible. But their failures with men are in fact primary and offstage. They have failed to measure up to the standards set by male mentors and rivals in legitimate jobs. The attention they seek from women is a poor substitute. They seek respect in private life, when it can really be won only in public, in the workplace.[38]

Poverty as Disorder. "Poverty" connotes something economic, but in an affluent society it really reflects a breakdown of order. Today's urban poverty arose chiefly because the disciplines of both work and family broke down in the mid-twentieth century among low-income people, especially blacks. Somehow, many parents lost their own commitment to jobs and spouses and thus their authority over children. Fathers failed to work and often disappeared. Their sons then became rootless, seeking to work but not knowing how. Paradoxically, the collapse came just as opportunities for blacks were expanding.

At the core of this breakdown was a loss of self-command among men and youth. As Daniel Patrick Moynihan wrote in 1965, "A community that allows a large number of young men to grow up in broken homes, dominated by women, never acquiring any stable relationship to male authority, never acquiring any set of rational expectations about the future—that community asks for and gets chaos."[39] If poverty means disorder, the chief solution to it is to restore order. Government must provide some of the pressure to work that today's poor have not internalized.

Assessing the Two Views. The economic approach goes far to explain the low wages of unskilled men. Even if these men work, the labor market does rate their services less highly than it once did. Culture cannot fully account for that. The wage problem is largely structural, and immigration has exacerbated it.

But economics explains inconsistent work a lot less well. At least low-paying jobs appear to be widely available. For low-skilled men to avoid them cannot be *economically* rational. In explaining nonwork, culture is preferable. It provides motives for low-skilled men to resist work where the economic theory does not. To these men, a life of poverty without steady work may indeed seem preferable to a life of work without respect.

This account is also more true to life. It captures the self-defeating quality of male nonwork, the confusion in these men's lives. One need not abstract from lifestyle and impute rational behavior to people on an "as if" basis, as the economic approach tends to do. We should believe what anecdotes and common observation suggest: on average, immigrants and women really are more tractable than low-skilled native-born men. That difference cannot be explained in economic terms.

The attempt of liberals since the 1960s to explain away nonwork by reference to various social barriers is not generally persuasive. But an older left's contention that capitalism was unfair to workers is still quite arguable. It is actually after men go to work, not before, that social barriers impede them most severely. Those with more education generally get better jobs than those with less.[40] The meritocracy has defined success in school as virtually the sole route to well-paid work. One must be at least a high school graduate to get a decent job, and the premium paid to college education is far greater. Those hurdles are too much for most disadvantaged men, even if they are ready and willing to work. And countermeasures to bolster unskilled wages, such as unionization or regulation, have sharply receded.

A key issue is whether reduced opportunities generate an oppositional culture or the reverse.[41] Both may be true. To say that lousy jobs directly generate resistance to working is too simple. That view does not account for trends over time. Work attitudes among the low skilled seem to have deteriorated in the period since the 1960s, an era when opportunities for minorities, on balance, improved. Work behavior among low-skilled men is worse today than it was under Jim Crow. That change must have causes outside the labor market.[42]

Yet, to a degree bad behavior and lousy jobs may reinforce each other. Acting out undermines men's reputation with employers, driving wages and opportunities down. At the same time, low wages exacerbate a dysfunctional culture. When disadvantaged men confront the job market, they may already be unfit for it, but low wages also dramatize their failure. This helps to trigger the cycle of rebellion and rejection, and that—more than low wages per se—is what brings them down.

Benefit-Oriented Programs

A review of past programs aimed at low-skilled men and youth confirms that work levels cannot be raised just by reducing economic barriers. Although benefits in many forms have been offered to these men, sometimes with good effects, none has clearly raised work levels, which is our focus here. The most effective programs also seek to change conduct.

Wage Subsidies. If one believes the economic theory, one way to motivate more work is to raise the minimum wage. Congress last did this in 2007. The final increase from that legislation took effect in July 2009, when the minimum reached $7.25 an hour. The threshold might well be raised further. Fifteen states and the District of Columbia already set higher minimums, the highest being $8.55 an hour in Washington State.[43] The main objection to raising the minimum wage is that doing so deters hiring the low skilled. In addition, most of the workers who would benefit are already above the poverty level, chiefly because they live in households where other people are working.

Most analysts would prefer to raise wage subsidies, which do not deter hiring and are better targeted to the low-income. Some propose paying noncustodial fathers a subsidy like the generous earned income tax credit (EITC) that is now paid to custodial parents of children—as much as 40 percent of wages—provided the fathers pay their child support.[44] Some would expand the much smaller federal EITC already given to single low-wage workers, with or without a connection to child support. A related device is to limit the child support a poor absent father must pay, for instance by limiting arrears, on the view that this "tax" deters working. I generally support such steps, which are discussed further in chapters 8 and 9.

But subsidies do not suffice to raise work levels. Higher wages would no doubt make poor men better off in some sense. They could either make more money if they worked or make the same money as now by working less. But whether they would work more, which is the goal here, is less clear. Work incentives in welfare operate like wage subsidies in that they allow welfare mothers to keep part of their welfare if they work, rather than have all earnings deducted from their grants. But before the 1990s, these provisions never affected whether mothers worked.[45] During the 1990s, the EITC appeared to increase work by single mothers, but its influence is difficult to separate from rising work requirements in welfare and a strong economy, which also drove the mothers' employment up.[46] And this finding applies largely to women rather than to men.

Federal income maintenance experiments from the 1960s through the 1980s showed that low-paid work effort was largely unresponsive to work incentives. If anything, work levels fell, and this was true for both men and women. The reason might be that, as mentioned above, raising wages creates offsetting incentives, both to raise and to lower work levels.[47] Or it might be simply that low-income workers are less responsive to incentives than economists suppose.

Experimental programs aimed at increasing employment among disadvantaged men have not found that raising wages has much effect. The New Hope project of the 1990s, which tested the effects of a work guarantee and work supports such as child care, increased the work and earnings of men outside families only "sporadically." And the program involved benefits besides wage subsidies as well as encouragement from a capable staff.[48] Jobs Plus, which ran from 1998 to 2003, tested whether financial incentives and social supports would increase work rates in public housing projects. The results showed some employment gains by men, but these were primarily husbands in two-parent welfare families, including many immigrants, not the more detached men who typify the male employment problem. Again, the program offered more than higher wages; it included various activities to promote more employment.[49] Statistical studies find that ensuring "good" jobs for men can produce steadier work among some men but worse behavior among others.[50]

One risk of higher pay is that it would make working in America even more attractive for foreigners than it already is. That would exacerbate the inflow of immigrants, thus creating even more competitors for low-skilled men in getting jobs. Wage enhancements might be limited to native workers, but illegal immigrants would falsely claim to be native. The danger could be avoided only if border and administrative controls on immigration became more effective than they are now.

Raising wages might increase work over the long term because of the interaction with culture, as already mentioned. Paying poor men more is a visible sign that society values their labor. Over time, that might reconcile some men to taking menial jobs. But in the short term, higher pay is insufficient to overcome the fractious psychology that now undermines male work. For wage incentives to have more effect on behavior, low-skilled men would first have to become the more routine, committed workers imagined in economic theory. At that point, they would start behaving more like trade unionists who bargain over work conditions. Higher wages alone cannot produce that shift. Today the chief value of higher pay may be political—in reconciling liberal leaders and opinion makers to the need to require men to work.

Education. Most disadvantaged men do badly in school. Many drop out, and few earn more than a high school diploma. How might policymakers help them stay in school longer, acquire better skills, and thus merit higher pay? Most schools in low-income areas function poorly. Government has recently tried to improve them by imposing outside standards, as in the federal No Child Left Behind Act of 2001, and by promoting choice and competition among schools. But teacher unions resist these steps, and better teachers and principals must be developed, so progress will necessarily be slow.

The alternative is to promote learning outside of the schools. Intensive preschool programs can raise employment and depress unwed pregnancy and crime in the later lives of students. Recently, some after-school programs for at-risk teenagers have shown promising effects on education and health.[51] But these benefits were seen in a few small, high-quality experiments. Such programs probably could not be expanded to a wider population and realize the same gains. The national Head Start program has not shown the same impacts achieved by the most noted preschool pilots. And even if these programs were effective at scale, their benefits would be long delayed.

Training. The final benefit-only approach to the work problem has been to train low-skilled workers as adults.[52] With the exceptions noted below, these programs have had smaller impacts than the work programs that transformed welfare. An evaluation of the Job Training Partnership Act during the 1990s found only slight earnings gains for adult men—5 percent—and losses for male youth. Gains in employment were 4 percent for adult men.[53] One reaction is that the programs are simply underfunded.[54] Another explanation—more plausible in my view—is that the clients commonly lack the capacity to raise their skills by much. The only way to elevate their wages, then, will be through regulating or subsidizing wages, as suggested above.[55] The main goal must be to get men working in low-skilled jobs so they can qualify for the subsidies.

In the cultural view, voluntary training has accomplished little because of the widespread misconception that the main barrier to work is low skills. In fact, it is work discipline. When men are poor in America, it is more often because they do not work consistently at *any* job than that they work steadily at low pay. That has been apparent since the 1960s.[56] What trainers really need to instill in disadvantaged men is the personal organization to get and stick with the jobs they can already get. If men show discipline, then employers will teach them specific skills. That is what immigrants typically show more of today than their native-born competitors. So, like education, improved training can make only a limited contribution to solving the male work problem.

The Need for Structure

Opportunity-oriented measures alone can do little to improve men's work effort because they fail to confront the oppositional culture described above. Nonworking men must comply with legitimate demands to work, however hard that is, before they can expect to earn the success and respect they crave. They must accept the old-fashioned view that the best expression of male dignity is to do a legitimate job, however lowly, rather than not to do it. Only this change can halt the current negative cycle, where resistance begets failure. Only this can begin a positive cycle, where better discipline yields steadier employment and advancement.

The solution suggested by welfare reform is that government must enforce work as well as promote it. Work must become an obligation, not a choice. Programs must link help and hassle. New benefits can assist, but they must be tied to definite requirements bearing on the clients. Some chance for success—some respect—must be offered up front. But there must also be demands to work steadily at the jobs offered or available, backed up by some kind of sanction.

Directive Programs. To raise work levels, programs must be directive. They must tell their clients clearly that they are expected to work. Programs framed as incentives or as additions to human capital leave work too much as a choice. Welfare reform mandated work for welfare mothers as a condition of aid. The most successful welfare work programs use case managers to check up on clients to be sure they fulfill their obligations, a style I call paternalist.[57]

In many areas of social policy, the most successful programs show this style. They tell their clients firmly what is expected of them, rather than leaving conduct open. The most dramatic example may be charter schools that have succeeded in teaching disadvantaged, often minority, students. They focus intensely on maintaining academic standards and enforcing good behavior generally because any disorder distracts from learning. Such schools appear to turn around the lives of many youth who otherwise might well become welfare mothers or nonworking fathers.[58]

Among innovative high schools aimed at noncollege students, the one clear success has been Career Academies, a form of school-within-a-school where teachers engage small groups of students. Instructors set high standards and then help youth attain them with more sustained and personalized attention than they get in the usual high school. This approach significantly improves students' earnings and employment, although educational outcomes are little affected.[59]

While Career Academies use the regular schools, Job Corps places disadvantaged youth in a prep-school-like setting, away from home, where they are closely supervised. Here the clearest gains are in educational credentials and reduced crime. Employment and earnings gains occur as well, but they are sustained only for the oldest youth in the program.[60]

These programs are for youth. Government has so far failed to generate comparable structures for adult men on the same scale. Such programs must be both more supportive and more demanding than traditional training. Rather than just imparting skills, they must address the troubled relations that disadvantaged men often have with employers. The program itself must model a constructive relationship between the worker and authority, trading acceptance for performance.

One model might be the Center for Employment Training (CET), a noted training agency for adults in San Jose, California. Local employers work closely with the center to define well-paying jobs they need to fill. The program then prepares trainees, most of whom are Hispanic, to take the jobs with full-day sessions that mimic actual work. The key appears to be offering real opportunities while keeping clients under pressure—with help from the surrounding Hispanic community—not to waste their opportunity. Unfortunately, CET has not proved to be replicable in other locations.[61]

Family welfare generally supports only single mothers with children, but intact families may also qualify in most states if the family is needy. In AFDC, the predecessor of TANF, unemployed fathers in these families were subject to work tests, and in some work programs they showed gains in employment and earnings.[62]

The Military Model. Except for the welfare work programs, all of the above programs are voluntary and cannot literally enforce work. Clients can walk away from them without losing anything else of value. The programs thus depend on informal suasions to maintain involvement. How could men be *required* to work in the same manner as welfare mothers?

Some observers see the military as a possible answer. Hugh Price is a successful black lawyer and former head of the National Urban League. He remarks on the power of military service to straighten out other blacks he knew growing up who never connected with school. The army imposed discipline while also offering advancement to soldiers who performed. It taught what society wants all youth to learn—that "if you do a job well, you get ahead." During the late 1980s, after conditions for ghetto youth had sharply deteriorated, another expert opined that it might be time to "conscript them for their own good."[63]

The military achieves exactly the sublimation of assertiveness that men need to succeed. The "four-star general," as Moynihan wrote in the Moynihan Report, expresses the "very essence of the male animal," which is "to strut," but it is in service to the nation. The military offers blacks an arena for advancement where equal opportunity is strictly enforced. Once in the military, many youth find that officers act like the fathers they never had, demanding compliance with rules and orders.[64] So the effect on black recruits can be salutary. Black entry into the military in the 1960s was high.

Unfortunately, relatively few blacks tested well enough to qualify for the army even in 1965, when the draft was still in force. Even fewer can do so today, when the military is volunteer and seldom admits high school dropouts. Some studies find that black men who serve in the military do indeed have better work records after service than blacks who do not, but black enlistment is no longer unusually high.[65] The utility of the military model for civilian programs today is largely in restructuring education and training programs for the disadvantaged. Even if these programs remain voluntary, strictly speaking, they may still generate unusual authority due to their military style.

The military appears to be effective at training and upgrading the skills of enlistees with deficits in literacy and numeracy. Trainers seem to succeed because they stress belonging, teamwork, motivation, and self-discipline. The ethos is that every youngster can succeed and that the whole person must be developed. Curricula are aimed at deficits in basic skills, and there is strong oversight, feedback, and accountability. At the same time, there are rewards, recognition, and promotion for those who measure up. Not everyone can adjust to such a structured approach, but the military appears to succeed with many disordered youth where the schools have failed.[66]

The potential can be seen in the Youth Challenge Program, a quasi-military youth training program developed by the National Guard. This is an intensive, residential reconditioning program akin to Job Corps. It removes youth to military bases for five months where they undergo a routine similar to army basic training. They keep a military schedule with very little unstructured time. The main emphasis is on remedial academic training, but the youth also receive physical training and instruction in health and other life skills. They are closely monitored by staff, who expect compliance and impose penalties for misbehavior. The clash with the youth's earlier life is often sharp. Those lasting the five months are then mentored for a year by a member of the local National Guard. Not all entrants stay the course, but those who do emerge with a far more realistic view of what it takes to succeed. Over about two years, this program has shown strong positive impacts on educational credentials and, to a lesser extent, on employment.[67]

Similar to successful charter schools, military academies maintain a close focus on standards and order. What academies add is an internal chain of command among the students themselves. Clear standards are set for promotion to the next rank, typically requiring solid (if not outstanding) grades, good discipline, and recommendations from teachers. The idea is to "co-opt disruptive students" and generate "peer pressure to behave."[68]

Conclusion

Raising poor men's work levels, like welfare mothers', will require some combination of help and hassle. Something must be done to raise unskilled wages, but as argued in the introduction, the instinct to respond only with generosity must be resisted. Higher rewards alone will not produce higher work levels, given the psychological freight these men bring to employment. There must also be some new effort to enforce work.

To rely only on benefits and opportunities presumes that the dysfunctions in men's lives result mainly from outside pressures. Push back those barriers, many say, and poor adults will begin to function. Even behavioral patterns that seem self-defeating will abate once there is hope. For people who feel powerless, the way forward is to give back control.[69] It sounds logical, and certainly improved benefits and opportunities must be part of any solution. But this strategy presumes that poor adults have the self-command that they typically lack. Even when opportunities are improved, a disorderly lifestyle must still be curbed before these men can take hold in the labor market and advance. So obligations to work, not just better chances, appear indispensible.

Programs that impose structure, as well as offer opportunity, have the best chance to generate steadier employment. One might assume from the male drive for respect that a hands-off, voluntary approach would be indispensible. Anything more directive would spark resistance. It is true that directive programs do alienate some men and youth. Yet despite this, authoritative programs still seem to perform best. The military consistently chooses to face down fractious behavior rather than tolerate it. People in authority confront men out of control and demand that they comply. Male assertiveness is turned around so that it supports rather than undercuts discipline. The message is that men are to assert their manhood by excelling within a demanding structure, rather than defying it. In the end, that is what many nonworking men need, even what they want.

The programs we have reviewed are not strictly mandatory, and most of them are aimed at youth. On both counts, work programs for older men might have advantages. Men who owe child support or are on parole can be obligated to work as most men or youth cannot. Older men should also respond better to mandatory work programs than youth. In Job Corps, it was the oldest youth who most clearly had employment gains, and in work programs for ex-offenders, older men have gained more than younger.[70]

Most existing directive programs have been based in the schools or the voluntary training system. To reach seriously nonworking men, however, new programs must be grafted onto the institutions that already deal with them—the child support and criminal justice systems. To these we now turn.

3

Child Support Enforcement

Next only to nonwork by parents, the leading cause of poverty in America is the breakup or nonformation of families. When parents split, family income inevitably drops. The mothers may still be able to work and avoid poverty, but often little more. Few families attain middle-class status without both parents working and contributing to the support of children.

Welfare reform recognized the importance of family breakup. PRWORA opened with loud statements about the importance of marriage for a healthy society. But aside from giving bonuses to states that reduced unwed pregnancy, the act did little actually to promote stronger families. It raised poor mothers' work levels—a critical success—but left unsolved the absence of fathers. Programs able to promote stronger families are still distant.

The child support system has operated as second-best, a way to get the spouse who is absent to help support the family. The absent or noncustodial parent, typically the father, is supposed to admit paternity of the children and pay a set amount to help support them. Some policymakers on both the right and the left have imagined that this system could sustain broken families in place of welfare. The federal requirement that states try to collect child support and so minimize welfare goes back to mandates that a conservative Senate Finance Committee first enacted in 1975.

Work requirements were the chief lever that drove the welfare rolls down in the 1990s, yet child support played an important secondary role.[1] Child support lifted 331,000 families off TANF in 2004, equivalent to 16 percent of the welfare caseload, and by one estimate it kept about half a million children out of poverty.[2] Mothers receiving child support are more likely to leave welfare and less likely to reenter it than those without. The chances that mothers leave welfare and decline to reenter it are also much higher in states that enforce child support rigorously.[3]

Efforts to improve collections initially stressed more effective enforcement on men already working. That approach made important gains, but it cannot solve the failure of many men to work and pay regularly. There are economic and cultural approaches to solving that problem, just as there are to the men's work program in general. The incentives approach has seen only limited success. Instead, a new approach seems required, one that will combine more effective enforcement with new efforts to help nonpaying men work. I review here past programs for which we have evidence of their effects. Well-crafted work programs tied to child support can help raise work levels.

Improving Enforcement

Child support's history is a struggle to get absent fathers to pay what they owe.[4] The system arose initially from civil law processes in which parents who divorced or separated arranged for the support of children. The departing spouse, usually the father, agreed to pay some amount to the custodial parent, usually the mother. If he did not pay, the system assumed that the mother could and would go after him in court. The child support system thus assumed from an early point that the father could pay and the chief problem was to force him to do so.

Stiffening Enforcement. Congressional conservatives seized on child support as a way to stem the rapid growth in welfare costs and caseloads in the 1960s and 1970s due to rising family breakup. Under the 1975 legislation, a new Title IV-D was added to the Social Security Act, and offices of Child Support Enforcement (CSE) were established at the federal and state levels. This was to provide the administrative resources and authority to pursue support without waiting for welfare mothers to take the initiative. As a condition of support, the mothers were to cooperate with CSE in locating absent fathers. Since then, the federal government has paid most of the cost of state collection efforts, subject to performance standards backed up by fiscal incentives. Currently, Washington pays 66 percent of states' collection costs and about $500 million in incentive funding.[5]

Since the initial legislation, the following advances have tightened up the enforcement of support:

- *Establishing paternity:* Determining the identity of the father of an abandoned child used to be a protracted and legalistic process. It has become more routine since the 1980s because the federal government has pressed states to adopt simpler, less judicial procedures. Moreover, in 1993, states were required to establish programs by which fathers could acknowledge paternity in the hospital soon after the birth of a child, and these have been notably successful.

- *Establishing orders:* Following paternity, setting the child support order for the father's payment was similarly legalistic, with judges often arbitrary or lenient. In 1984 and 1988, Washington made states establish guidelines for orders that judges ordinarily had to follow. Orders are supposed to be reassessed every three years.

- *Collecting support:* Originally, absent fathers controlled paying their orders, and they might not do so regularly. But since the 1984 and 1988 legislation, states have had to implement automatic wage withholding, whereby child support, like taxes, is automatically deducted from fathers' paychecks. This practice sharply increased collections.

- *Establishing interstate enforcement:* Getting child support set and paid was particularly difficult when the father left the family for a different state. But progress has been made by mandating common procedures. Data systems at the federal level help locate fathers no matter where they live.

By all these means, enforcement has improved greatly in the last twenty years. Fathers now usually cannot evade all payment, at least if they work in the regular economy. In states and localities with strong administration, it is now possible to get something from a large majority of fathers who owe support. One exemplar is Racine County, Wisconsin, which has made enforcement a specialty. There a large staff pursues nonpayers relentlessly, bringing hundreds of enforcement actions every week. As one manager proudly told me, "We take control."[6]

Traditionally, CSE ignored low-skilled men because they were hard to find and had little money in any event. This was one reason why nonworking men became such a problem. But today the system can at least get most of these men to participate in work programs, if not to pay regularly. In the Parents' Fair Share (PFS) demonstration, detailed below, around 70 percent of clients referred either paid up or participated as directed, and most of those who did not were referred back to CSE for noncompliance.[7] So, today, government *can* get control. The question is what to do with it.

Table 3-1 shows that, since 1978, prodigious increases have occurred in paternities and awards established, far outpacing the growth in population. In constant dollars, child support collections nearly doubled between 1978 and 2005. By 2001, these monies comprised 17 percent of income in the families receiving them—30 percent for families in poverty.[8] And whereas in 1978 only 38 percent of poor mothers had a child support award and 18 percent received some payment, by 2005 those figures had jumped to 54 and 45 percent, respectively. Mothers above the poverty line were doing only slightly better, with figures of 64 and 45 percent, respectively.

Limits to Enforcement. Conventional enforcement has run into diminishing returns. As table 3-1 shows, even in 2005, about half of poor mothers had no support order and received no support. And for all mothers, only a quarter received all that was due them, a figure that has improved little since 1978. Despite the increase in collections, some $12 billion in child support due went uncollected in 2005.

The enforcement problem is not primarily that fathers pay too little support once working. Rather, it is that they pay nothing at all because they have escaped paternity and order establishment or they are not working, or not in a legal job. Besides further progress on paternity, the key to raising collections is getting men into regular jobs subject to withholding. As one child support lawyer said to me, "If they're working, they're paying." In this the support problem resembles poverty in general: adults are poor principally because they fail to work regularly at *any* job, not because their wages are low.

OCSE realizes that its highly automated collection systems alone cannot solve the enforcement problem. It believes that many nonpaying fathers have resources to pay that they do not admit. Hence the office states, "We

TABLE 3-1
CHILD SUPPORT TRENDS, 1978–2005

	1978	1989	1999	2005
Paternities established (in thousands)	111	339	1,600	1,630
Awards established (in thousands)	315	936	1,220	1,180
All eligible women				
Percent awarded support	59	58	62	61
Percent received payment	35	37	40	42
Percent received full payment	24	26	25	25
Women above poverty				
Percent awarded support	67	65	66	64
Percent received payment	41	43	45	45
Women below poverty				
Percent awarded support	38	43	52	54
Percent received payment	18	25	27	45
Payments (billions of 2005 dollars)				
Child support due	19	25	35	35
Child support received	12	17	21	22
Deficit	7	8	14	12
Collections under Title IV-D as percent of all collections	23	47	84	93

NOTES: "All eligible women" means single mothers with own children under age twenty-one. Some numbers do not add due to rounding.
SOURCE: U.S. Congress, House Committee on Ways and Means, *2008 Green Book: Background Material, and Data on the Programs within the Jurisdiction of the Committee on Ways and Means* (Washington, DC: U.S. Government Printing Office, 2008), tables 8.8, 8.10.

need to . . . develop and utilize tools other than wage withholding to enforce these orders." This effort will require much closer monitoring of cases, including more adjustments of obligations to pay, both up and down, and the ability to "immediately intervene when child support is not paid." Such reasoning leads directly toward the support enforcement programs that we consider below.[9]

Approaches to Enforcement

In approaching the enforcement problem, we encounter the same two approaches seen in chapter 2—economics versus culture.

Economics. The economics approach asserts that the main reason absent fathers do not pay all they could is that it is not in their interests to do so. If families are poor, fathers can free ride on welfare, which will normally support their dependents for them. The belief that fathers reasoned like this generated much of the impetus to create Title IV-D in the first place. To impute economic logic like this has long been a staple of conservative criticisms of welfare.[10]

Even if the father does pay support, he has an incentive not to do so through the official system. If he pays support openly, the government will pocket most of it to repay the cost of welfare. The family's grant will be reduced by any support received, thus leaving it no better off than before. Poor fathers and mothers thus have an interest in arranging payment unofficially between themselves so that all the money goes to the family and welfare is unaffected. Each parent may also believe that this way he or she has more control over the other person. The father can pay in kind—diapers, baby bottles, and so forth—so that he knows his contribution will benefit his children, not just the mother, while the mother can threaten to turn the father in to child support authorities should he fail to pay. Although in theory the mother must cooperate with collection as a condition of aid, in practice she can deny that she knows who the father is or his whereabouts.[11]

To change the incentives, Congress in 1984 mandated that at least $50 per month of any child support collected go to the family, net of any reductions in welfare. This was to give both parents a reason to channel payments through the official system. But the incentive was costly to states. The requirement was eliminated by PRWORA, and most states reverted to claiming all collections for themselves, at least for the diminishing numbers of cases that had been on welfare or Medicaid.

PRWORA also allowed states to pass through more than $50 to the families if they chose. Wisconsin, as part of its dramatic welfare reform, passed through *all* collections made without reducing welfare at all. An evaluation showed that both the share of fathers paying support and the amount they paid increased. However, the gains were small, usually 4 to 6 percent, although they were higher for new cases not previously on welfare.[12]

When TANF was reauthorized in 2006, Congress allowed states to pass through as much as $100 a month in collections ($200 for a family with two or more children) without having to reimburse the federal government for its share of those recoveries. Nevertheless, changing incentives are clearly insufficient to solve the payment problem.

Culture. The economics approach assumes that nonpaying fathers are able to pay should they find it in their interest. That also is the traditional assumption of the child support system, but it is far from true. We assume that low-skilled fathers are much better off than their spouses, who have children to support. But the poverty rate of noncustodial fathers aged 18–34 is virtually the same as that of young custodial mothers—37 versus 38 percent. About a third of these fathers pay their child support as directed, a third do not pay and could, and a third do not pay and could not do so without impoverishing themselves. These poor nonpayers—dubbed "turnips" rather than deadbeats—represent the core of the enforcement problem.[13]

Also, the economic approach presumes that men are serving their self-interest when they fail to pay. But for poor fathers and mothers to evade the official system does not really serve their interests. The father gets no credit toward his child support obligation, allowing his arrears to build, while the mother has to lie to the welfare system, which risks denying the family needed benefits. The attitudes of both parents are also full of misconceptions. Some fathers believe that the mother, not the state, creates their child obligation, and in the days of the $50 requirement some mothers thought that $50 was all that the father paid.[14] Neither parent has conducted the relationship rationally, often becoming parents and breaking up without serious consideration.

The child support problem reflects a larger disarray. The typical poor mother and father tend to have orthodox goals for their family, but—typical of the culture of poverty—neither feels much responsibility for realizing those norms. Mothers feel put upon because they have to take care of children with little help from the father, while the father feels overwhelmed by the mother's demands and, even more, by those of employment. Low-income fathers find themselves unable to work regularly, but they blame

employers or the labor market. They expect that their child support obligations should be reduced accordingly, but the system is not that responsive.
Typically, neither parent supports the system, the mothers viewing it as ineffective and the fathers as unfair.[15]

Poor fathers search desperately for income to meet the many demands
on them. They strain to get something from the mother, or government, or
employers. Helping to meet their needs must be part of any solution, but
the fundamental problem is these men's lack of self-command. Kay
Hymowitz remarks:

> One of the most striking things about talking to poor inner-city
> men is their sense of drift; life is something that happens to them.
> I asked several men where they would like to see themselves in
> ten years; all of them gave me a puzzled, I-never-really-thought-
> about-it look. Both marriage and vocation are part of the project
> that is the deliberate pursuit of a meaningful and connected life.
> To put it a little differently, to marry and to earn a living are to try
> to master life and shape it into a coherent narrative.[16]

A lack of direction defines these men. They often give offense or incur obligations without realizing what they are doing. Until they acquire more ability to avoid trouble and to satisfy others, they cannot expect much reward
out of life.

How to help them start putting out when they begin with nothing—that
is the problem social policy must solve. It will not be solved just by crack-
ing down, as child support enforcement has traditionally done. That course
might simply drive nonpaying men further away from their responsibilities
and the legal economy.

Enforcement Programs

Rather, the child support system needs a more complex strategy that links
better enforcement with more practical help and, above all, more supervision. Low-income men, like welfare mothers, need case managers able to
both help them fulfill their responsibilities and insist that they do so.

Child support work programs emerged to overcome the difficulty child
support judges have in overseeing such men. When noncustodial parents

do not pay their judgments, those with regular jobs are the easiest to deal with. Their employers can be found and their wages garnished. In most cases they have too much to lose to resist enforcement. A poor nonpayer, however, typically has a lot less to lose and is tougher to get a grip on. Dragged before a judge, he typically claims to lack a job and income. The judge cannot easily verify these claims. He can order the father to make a one-time "purge payment" toward his arrears, but this does not establish what he could pay on a regular basis. He can also tell the father to get a job, but when he reappears in several months he can still say he is jobless, and the judge will hesitate to hold him in contempt.

The judge can, however, remand him to a work program. Unlike getting a job, that is an obligation the father cannot evade. Now he must show up or pay his judgment—or go to jail for contempt. If he is working surreptitiously, participation will conflict with his unreported job and force him to pay up. If he really is jobless, the program can help him to find work. Either way, he cannot avoid all responsibility.[17]

State Programs. Such programs began to emerge on a wide scale in the 1980s as localities grappled with the enforcement problem. A few of these became nationally visible: Children First was enacted in 1987 in Wisconsin as one of that state's early welfare reform initiatives. It was implemented in 1990 in Racine and Fond de Lac, both leading counties in support enforcement, and was later expanded to thirty-nine of Wisconsin's seventy-two counties. The program initially assigned clients to community service positions (work in government or nonprofit agencies), but after 1993 it offered training and other services as well. With other funding, Racine also offered basic education and a "parental responsibility class" that confronted fathers with their duties to their children. Some of that funding came from the fatherhood programs mentioned below. The program remained small due to limited funding. In 1999–2001, it was able to fund only 2,850 slots, although counties managed to serve as many as 4,958 clients in 2000 using other monies.[18]

The Non-Custodial Parent Choices (NCP Choices) program appeared in Texas beginning in 2005. An adjunct of the state's Choices work program for welfare mothers, NCP Choices targets nonpaying fathers whose families are currently or formerly on welfare. These fathers are assigned to the program by local judges on the recommendation of child support administrators. The fathers must fulfill their judgments, join the program, or go to jail—in the state's phrase, "Pay, play, or pay the consequences." Men in the program are served by special staff at the Texas Workforce Commission (TWC), the state's chief training agency. Funding is from TANF monies channeled through the TWC. The emphasis is on job search and placement in existing jobs, with minimal training. To minimize job losses, NCP Choices also follows up on clients for six months after they are placed in jobs. NCP Choices was implemented in five counties in 2005 and another four in 2007.

Like Children First, NCP Choices is small relative to its potential client pool. In the ten counties used for the evaluation described below, the program enrolled 2,296 clients, compared to 522,689 noncustodial parents not in the program. At the time of my interviews in February 2009, the program had 3,194 clients statewide. Nevertheless, even at its present scale, NCP Choices appears to be the largest child support enforcement program in the country, covering 75 percent of the state population.[19]

Parents' Fair Share. Parents' Fair Share (PFS) was a national demonstration that the Manpower Demonstration Research Corporation (MDRC), the noted evaluation firm, conducted between 1992 and 1996 at seven sites in different states. The goal was to create a new structure for child support enforcement that could not only increase collections but also improve absent fathers' employment and earnings and their relationships with their families.

PFS was more complex than either Children First or NCP Choices. Child support agencies were supposed to pay closer attention to the support orders of clients than they were used to doing, modifying them more quickly as the men's circumstances changed. Most sites reduced or remitted clients' child support judgments as long as the clients were in the program to give them an incentive to participate. The employment services included on-the-job training as well as job search. The program also offered mediation services to try to reconnect fathers with their spouses and children, and it organized peer support groups at which participants could discuss their problems with each other.

PFS had trouble enrolling enough clients in the program, although they were ordered into it by child support judges. The program's seven sites each had several thousand child support cases involving welfare, yet it was able to enroll only 5,460 from all of them, even after special outreach efforts.[20]

Fatherhood Programs

Besides child support work programs aimed at enforcement, there have also been "fatherhood" programs aimed more at helping low-skilled men and their families deal with their problems. These honored the child support obligation but stressed it less.

In part, the fatherhood movement was a reaction against the perceived one-sidedness of child support. Fathers—especially blacks—saw that system as allied with their estranged spouses, with its sole purpose of getting as much money out of them as possible. They often received nothing in return, not even visitation rights. Mothers and children already received much more support and attention from government than poor men, and now the enforcers were on their side as well.[21]

The fathers had a point. The groups that pushed the development of child support have been family oriented. In the 1950s and 1960s, social workers saw the system as a way to get more money for needy families, while in the 1970s conservatives saw it as an alternative to welfare. Feminists espoused it as a way of defending women against men who abandoned them. To all these groups, absent fathers were at best invisible and at worst the culprits who should simply be made to pay. Only later did fathers' groups arise to demand attention to men's own problems—one of which was the rising pressure of child support enforcement.[22]

Whereas the child support programs were sponsored by public agencies, the fatherhood programs were typically run by nongovernmental organizations with ties to minority communities, with public agencies in a more peripheral role. In place of public funding, several programs received outside foundation grants, with the Ford Foundation often the lead donor. The most important fatherhood programs to date were the following:

- *Teen Fathers Collaboration* (1983–85): Served teenage fathers at eight sites. Agencies had served mothers and children and now sought out the fathers also. Services included General Educational Development preparation, training, job placement, parenting, and counseling. The purpose was partly to advocate on behalf of the fathers and to counter myths about them. Funded by Ford and community foundations.

- *Young Unwed Fathers Project* (1991–93): Operated at six sites serving fathers under age twenty-five. Offered education and training to develop the youth as fathers and workers. Assisted with establishing paternity and paying support. Provided case management for up to eighteen months, even after job placement. Most fathers participated voluntarily. Funded by the U.S. Departments of Agriculture and Labor and several foundations.

- *Responsible Fatherhood Programs* (1998–2000): Operated at eight sites serving jobless and underemployed fathers. Offered services to increase their employment and earnings, promote more involved parenting, and motivate compliance with child support. Clients were partly volunteers and partly ordered to participate by judges. Funded by the U.S. Department of Health and Human Services.

- *Welfare-to-Work Grants Program* (1998–2000): Served hardest-to-employ TANF recipients and noncustodial fathers of children on welfare. Emphasized employment but also increasing child support payments and improving fathers' relationships with families. Men who participated were partly volunteers and partly ordered to participate by courts. Some programs focused on fathers on parole or probation. Funded by the U.S. Department of Labor.

- *Partners for Fragile Families* (2000–2003): At thirteen sites, aimed to serve young fathers under age twenty-five, while they still had a relationship with their spouses and had not accumulated large child support arrears. Promoted voluntary establishment of paternity, payment of child support, maintaining ties to families, as well as employment and training. Funded by the U.S. Department of Health and Human Services, Ford, and other foundations.[23]

Even more than PFS, all the fatherhood programs had trouble recruiting clients. All were surprisingly small. The Young Unwed Fathers Project enrolled all of 459 men over three years. Partners for Fragile Families enrolled barely half the clients expected, and one of its sites in New York City had only thirty-seven enrollees.[24] Even though the programs were offering new benefits from which the fathers might gain, few men came forward on their own. This was one reason why most programs relied, at least partly, on mandatory referrals from CSE or the parole system.

Evaluations

All of the above programs delivered worthwhile services. But how do we know whether the clients gained anything from them? Evaluations are supposed to determine how much difference a program made to an outcome of interest such as employment—what evaluators call *impact*. That assessment requires allowing, or controlling, for other factors that affect the outcome. To do this, one constructs a "counterfactual"—an estimate of how the clients would have done on their own—and then compares this to how they did with the program.

Evaluation Design. The simplest evaluation design is the before-after comparison. One sees whether the clients did better after the program than they had done before. Here the counterfactual is the clients themselves prior to the program. By this standard, many of the child support programs appear successful. The men they served often worked more, earned more, and paid more child support after the program than they had done before. The trouble is that they might well have improved on their own, so before-after evaluations typically overstate impact.

A better design is the quasi-experiment. Here the clients are compared to similar men who are not served. If the clients improve more than the comparison group, we assume the difference is due to the program and not something else. But for the estimate to be valid, the program and comparison groups must be as similar as possible. It is fairly easy to make them similar in features that are readily measurable, such as gender, age, race, or education. But how do you control for differences that are not measurable, particularly in motivation? People who volunteer for a program may well be more determined to improve themselves than those who do not. If we then find that they outperform the unserved, some of that difference may be due to these unmeasured differences. When outcomes appear driven by who chooses to participate in a program, rather than by the services received, evaluators speak of "selection effects."

One good quasi-experimental approach defines the comparison group using propensity score matching. Each experimental client is compared to whichever member of the comparison group he or she most resembles. An impact is then inferred by comparing outcomes for the two groups. Done well, this method minimizes selection effects, but it does not eliminate them.

The gold standard in evaluation is the true experiment, based on random assignment. Here, people eligible for a program are assigned by chance to either an experimental group that gets the tested treatment or a control group that does not. Because assignment is random, we can assume that the experimental and control groups will differ very little in either measurable or unmeasurable ways, thus precluding selection effects. Unfortunately, random assignment is unpopular with program operators because not all people who apply for a program can be served. Some recent evaluations of men's programs have used propensity score matching as second-best.

Parents' Fair Share. The evaluation history for child support work programs is limited. Only one of the above programs received an experimental evaluation—Parents' Fair Share. Those results showed the following:

- *Large increases in services provided:* Many more clients became involved in various activities than did members of the control group. The program thus countered to some extent the isolation of low-income men from government. The most popular service was the peer support group.

- *Sizable gains in child support:* Closer monitoring of men's cases raised the share paying support, and also the amount they paid, by 8 percentage points or 16 percent, even prior to referral to PFS. There was a strong "smoke out" effect, with around a quarter of the clients admitting they had jobs. PFS itself raised the share paying support by a further 4 points or 5 percent but did not increase the size of payments.

- *Smaller gains in employment and earnings:* PFS showed no impacts on work or earnings levels overall, but it did show some gains for the more disadvantaged fathers, those who were high school dropouts or had not worked recently.

- *No improvement of family ties*: Despite its mediation services, PFS did not improve relationships between fathers and their families. Fathers' interactions with children increased only for fathers who began with the least contact. Ties with spouses appeared to be deeply troubled. Indeed, the program may have increased conflict.[25]

PFS showed, on balance, that child support is still best at its traditional function—getting more money out of absent fathers who work. It did not solve nonworking men's employment problems and their larger disengagement. For those problems, the child support system would need to enforce participation better and insist on more actual work, if necessary through the provision of guaranteed jobs in some form.[26]

State Programs. In an experimental evaluation in Racine County, Children First failed to show clear impacts. Clients in the program received more services than the controls, but it is unclear whether they emerged better off. The experiment, however, was compromised—some control group members as well as experimentals were served. Also, child support collections were rising sharply even for the control group because of the high performance already achieved in child support in Racine and Wisconsin generally. This set the bar high for the new program to show any impact.

However, counties like Racine that implemented Children First in its early years did tend to outperform counties that implemented it later or not at all. Thus, the program was one of several initiatives that led to superior child support enforcement over time. That at least suggests an impact. As with PFS, gains in child support payments appeared greater than in men's employment or earnings.[27]

NCP Choices received a statistical evaluation based on propensity score matching. As in PFS, there were large gains in services received, but somewhat stronger impacts. The share of the time that men in the program paid child support over a year rose by 14 percentage points or 47 percent, and the amount they paid monthly rose by $57 or 51 percent. The share of time men worked during a year rose by 8 points or 21 percent. Unexpectedly, quarterly earnings *fell* by $587 or 17 percent. That was probably because the program caused many lower-paid men to go to work, thus reducing average wages below those of the comparison group. All these are effects in the first year; effects persisted at somewhat reduced levels for two to four years total. Although gains were greatest when economic conditions were good, somewhat reduced effects occurred even when conditions were worse. The effect on employment was thus smaller than on support payments, as in PFS, but now the impact extended to the experimental group as a whole.[28]

On balance, the state programs probably outperformed PFS. The likely reason is that they focused more clearly on getting men to work and keep working in available jobs. Less time and attention was spent on the dimensions of PFS that appeared less successful—training for better jobs and improving relationships with families. In NCP Choices, child support obligations are not usually reduced while men were in the program.

Fatherhood Programs. The evaluations of the fatherhood programs are before-after at best. No assessments were done using comparison or control groups. I concentrate on the employment and child support results, although some of these programs also registered gains in education and other outcomes as well.

- *Teen Fathers Collaboration:* About two-thirds of young fathers served were jobless on entering the program. By the end, 61 percent of the jobless clients had obtained jobs, either full or part time. Forty-six percent of clients who were nongraduates and not in school at the outset had positive educational outcomes— entering a General Educational Development program or returning to school.[29]

- *Young Unwed Fathers Project:* Twenty-three percent of the young fathers were working at program entry; a year later, 54 percent were working, or more than double. Average wages grew by 20 percent, and the share of clients with a high school diploma or General Educational Development certificate grew by 23 percent.[30]

- *Responsible Fatherhood Programs:* The four sites with the lowest preprogram work levels realized gains of as much as 33 percentage points, but at three other sites there was no significant gain.

Four sites also recorded earnings growth from 25 to 250 percent, but at three others there was no change. There were some improvements in child support payments.[31]

- *Welfare-to-Work Grants Programs:* Over two years, clients' employment levels rose from very low levels to around 40 percent. Correspondingly, poverty rates fell by around 30 percentage points for those working. Wages grew modestly but remained low, around $8 an hour. We should note that most clients were hard-to-employ TANF recipients rather than men.[32]

- *Partners for Fragile Families:* At the time of the program, employment rates for clients were slightly over half, and they changed little during or after the program. Average quarterly earnings, however, grew from $1,501 at baseline to $2,907 two years later. That increase is almost a doubling, but from very low levels. Child support compliance increased more clearly, with orders and payments both growing.[33]

Some of these programs show their clients improving sharply in employment, earnings, and child support performance, but the improvement is always from low levels. And results are overshadowed by the participation problem. These programs all had few takers, with most of them volunteers, although some were referred by the courts. That is the situation where selection effects can be substantial. Thus, many of the improvements claimed probably would have occurred without the program.

Conclusion

Overall, the evaluations of the enforcement and fatherhood programs are encouraging, but no more than that. The better efforts—particularly PFS and NCP Choices—suggest that well-crafted work programs can at least reach enough nonpaying men to justify their costs, although no cost-benefit calculations were done to test this. Those impacts might be discernable to evaluators. Whether they can raise work levels in more visible ways, as welfare reform did, is less certain.

That difference reflects limited prior development and authority. By the time work programs began to impact welfare in the late 1980s, efforts to put welfare mothers to work were already twenty years old. Voluntary and benefit-oriented strategies had failed. It was clear that work had to be enforced as a condition of aid if work levels were to rise. Also, in some localities, politicians embraced that goal, and administrators had figured out how to achieve it. Some pioneer programs, such as those in San Diego and Riverside, California, and in Wisconsin, produced clear results, visible even without evaluations. Then other localities got on board, and finally the nation as a whole followed. In child support work efforts, in contrast, there is less experience and less commitment to change, and the best program model is less clear. As the fatherhood experience suggests, some programs are still protective of fathers and loath to enforce work.

As with welfare mothers, solutions for nonpaying men require the buildup of new institutions. Child support began as a narrowly legal arrangement among parties to a divorce. But since 1975, complexity has grown—first CSE, then work programs, and then the nongovernmental organizations serving fathers.[34] Progress lies chiefly in optimizing this emerging institutional system. We will encounter this same growth and spreading of structures in the criminal justice area.

4

Criminal Justice

The other great arena for men's work policy is criminal justice. The prison and parole systems, like child support, already have authority over many nonworking men. Like child support, they have helped to restore some order to low-income communities in recent decades. Data in chapter 1 showed that crime rates have fallen substantially since the early 1990s, although how much law enforcement contributed to this is unclear.

At the same time, the criminal justice world, like child support, harbors a growing sense of limitation. The reduction in crime has come at the expense of incarcerating more than 2 million Americans, a huge cost. Convicts are also returning home in large numbers—735,454 in 2008.[1] Past rehabilitation programs have failed to reintegrate ex-offenders, although they may make some contribution. Nor has the parole system reduced recidivism. The current hope is that prison reentry can be managed through community services so as to reduce crime and improve overall public safety.

In that quest, work programs figure prominently. As in child support, evaluations of these programs are limited, but the results are similar, suggesting some potential to raise work levels. The discussion below describes the criminal justice problem and the traditional responses to it, then goes on to the reentry movement and the recent work programs. My assessment, as above, is largely confined to programs for which we have some independent evidence of effects.

Responses to Crime

The sharp upturn in crime that hit the country after 1960 highlighted criminal justice and its failings. In part the explosion came from social changes, such as growing black assertiveness, the decline of the family, and the weakening of informal social restraints in the 1960s. But it also arose from institutional failings. Criminals no longer seemed deterred by the threat of "doing time." Nor did being imprisoned seem to improve their functioning. On release, they were likely to offend again. A government study found that in 1994, 30 percent of former inmates were rearrested for some new offense within six months, 59 percent within two years, and 68 percent within three years. Within three years, half of them were convicted of a new crime, and a quarter were back in prison.[2]

Most states had trusted criminal justice to handle crime with limited oversight. The probation system supervised lesser offenders in the community without sending them to prison. Serious offenders were sentenced to prison for indefinite periods. Of those incarcerated, some received rehabilitation meant to improve their skills and promote law-abidingness. When they were released turned on judgments by parole boards about when they were safe to return to society. Parolees were then supervised in the community by parole officers for the remainder of their sentences.

Rehabilitation. The crime explosion brought all these institutions into question. In a noted study, Robert Martinson concluded that "nothing works." That is, there was no evidence that rehabilitation programs, either in or out of prison, succeeded or that anything about prisons could change offenders for the better. It was preferable, then, to use prisons simply to deter offense and express society's disapproval of crime.[3]

Some experts think programs in prison meant to teach useful skills, reorient sexual behavior, and counter drug abuse can do some good, but the impact on recidivism will be perhaps 20 percent.[4] Overshadowing even these modest claims are weak evaluations. Most studies of programs are not based on random assignment. Evaluators tend to exaggerate impacts. They often work for the agency running the program, so assessments are not at arms length.[5]

Parole. Somehow, parole officers failed to prevent the repeat crimes that were helping to fill the prisons. Violent offenses by parolees created more fear and offense than the same crimes committed by people not on parole. The case of Willie Horton, spotlighted by George H. W. Bush's presidential campaign in 1988, comes immediately to mind. Conservatives attacked the system as too lenient—prisoners were being released too early, rendering their sentences meaningless. Liberals, for their part, found the system too arbitrary.

In response, parole officers shifted their focus from helping parolees toward protecting public safety. They became tougher about enforcing parole rules, such as keeping appointments and passing drug tests. Officers sent more parolees back to prison for breaking these rules. These "technical violations" grew to account for over a third of prison admissions. That contradicted the premise of parole, that it could supervise ex-offenders in the community and reduce incarceration.[6]

Parole would appear to involve the same kind of paternalistic oversight that has shown results in social programs in other areas, as noted in chapter 2. Yet parole has no clear effects on rearrests. That might be because it is not usually very intensive. Parole officers typically have caseloads of around seventy cases, who meet with them briefly only once or twice a month.[7] Yet even intensive parole supervision does not reduce crime. An experiment in 1986–91 in which caseloads were nineteen to forty parolees and officers interacted with them much more intensively led only to even more technical violations and returns to prison—not lower crime.[8] The problem most likely is that the demands parole makes on ex-offenders do not address their main problems. Supervision has to be redirected toward more constructive activities aimed at these problems.[9]

Due to the doubts about rehabilitation and parole, states curbed discretion. "Truth in sentencing" laws mandated that more sentences be fully served. Fourteen states abolished discretionary sentencing entirely. Parole more often became part of the original sentence, not determined on a flexible basis by parole boards. Today, 41 percent of ex-offenders are released from prison to mandatory parole, only 24 percent to discretionary parole. And 19 percent are released at the end of sentences with no parole at all, often the most dangerous offenders.[10]

Prison. Without clear alternatives, states responded to rising crime chiefly by incarcerating more offenders. The prisons grew due to more arrests and convictions but also because more convicts were sentenced to prison rather than lesser penalties and because sentences were lengthened. Many drug offenders were incarcerated who earlier would not have been. Effectively, the ideal of rehabilitation, which had dominated criminal justice for a century, was abandoned. The goals now were simply to express society's outrage at crime and to prevent and deter further offenses.[11]

However, politics eventually turned against the hard-line strategy. The strain on state budgets was considerable. While low-income communities want protection from crime, they are also disrupted when so many men are imprisoned—and when equally large numbers return. A movement to reassess imprisonment arose. The George W. Bush administration and some members of Congress, including conservatives, supported reentry programming, and, more recently, Democratic senator Jim Webb has proposed a national commission on criminal justice reform.[12]

Just as Bill Clinton promised to end welfare as we know it, leading to welfare reform, some reformers seek to end parole as we know it. The most radical proposal, from Martin Horn, would sharply curtail both incarceration and parole in their traditional forms. Prison would be used mainly for the most dangerous offenders. Recovery from crime would be sought mainly in the community. Parole's oversight role would be taken over largely by the police and its service role by nonprofit community organizations overseen by parole.[13]

The Appeal to Community

The discrediting of traditional policies prompted new strategies that appealed in different ways to the community. People and institutions outside the prisons and parole would now help solve the crime and rehabilitation problems.

Community Policing. The police had traditionally reacted to crime after the fact. They aimed to get to crime scenes quickly, gather information and witnesses, and detain suspects. But research showed that these tactics did not deter or reduce crime. In contrast, community policing aimed to forestall criminals rather than apprehend them. The police had to shift from pursuing offenders to maintaining order. Policing now would be decentralized to neighborhoods. Officers were to get out of their squad cars and walk beats in the traditional manner, getting to know neighborhoods. Rather than ignore minor "quality of life" offenses such as loitering or graffiti, they would focus on these. That gave a message about community values that preempted worse crimes. And, often, offenders detained for lesser offenses would turn out to have warrants outstanding for major ones.[14]

Whereas policing, like prisons and parole, had been largely self-contained, the new strategy sought support from civil society. By reconnecting to neighborhoods, the police tried to draw intelligence from outside law enforcement. Prosecutors sought to target the crimes that were most important to the community. Where crime tended to break down community, law enforcement tried to rebuild it, then call upon it to reduce crime. Recent reductions in crime, notably in New York City, appear to have come from this strategy.[15]

One spectacular success for this approach was the "Ceasefire" initiatives in Boston, Cincinnati, and other cities in the late 1990s. Drug gangs guilty of multiple murders had failed to respond to traditional enforcement methods. They did respond to clear-cut messages from the authorities that the killings had to stop or there would be certain consequences. The police, probation officers, and other agencies put more personnel on the streets, where they enforced probation rules and curfews. In Boston, they also drew on political support from local black clergy. Government and the community mobilized together to halt crime.[16] However, homicides later rebounded in Boston, probably because oversight of offenders weakened.[17]

Societies with low crime rates, such as Japan, enforce order overwhelmingly through informal suasions rather than government. The United States did much the same in the later nineteenth century, when the disorder of rapid urbanization was tamed largely by Sunday schools, the YMCA, and the temperance movement. The discrediting of "social control" after 1960 was one reason for the crime explosion.[18] Community policing resurrected social control, led this time by public authorities.

Prison Reentry. The prison reentry movement extends this same logic to the problem of ex-offenders. The idea is that rehabilitation programs in prisons may not achieve much because that environment is too removed from the real world. Another opportunity beckons when prisoners are released. The goal is not necessarily rehabilitating offenders in a complete sense, but simply forestalling future crime. The chance of recidivism is greatest in the months just after release, so reentry services should be "front-loaded." When ex-offenders leave prison, they should have a plan to reconnect with families, employment, and housing, and service providers should ensure that these connections are made.

With the new strategy, the criminal justice system becomes less autonomous. Community organizations now enter the prisons to help plan prisoners' transitions and then provide them with the required services on release. Parole officers might not be downgraded, as in Horn's proposals, but they would work alongside private bodies in serving the men, rather than largely on their own. The locale of rehabilitation shifts from prison or parole to a broader web of efforts in the community.[19]

As in community policing, authority is reconstituted and decentralized. Discretionary parole might be restored, lest offenders lose incentives to behave well while in prison.[20] But revocations of parole for technical violations would be reduced, replaced by lesser sanctions in the community. Parole might be combined with local probation. Judges might oversee reentry, on the model of drug courts. The reentry approach, Jeremy Travis writes, "takes community corrections officers out from behind their desks and places them directly in neighborhoods." In this "new world of supervision," ex-offenders face interaction not just with the parole system but with the police and the various agencies providing them services. "These initiatives are a far cry from traditional social work approaches to parole and probation. Anonymity is replaced with in-your-face contact."[21]

Prison Reentry Programs

Work programs for ex-offenders arose as part of this broader movement. Although employment is not reentry's only goal, it is a central one. Officials recognize that whether former offenders avoid repeat crime critically depends on whether they go to work. Past training or work programs for ex-offenders have not performed well, but some recent programs are more promising. These efforts resemble those we have already considered under child support.[22]

In general, prisons have prepared ex-offenders for employment mainly by putting them to work within the prisons. But only half of prisoners get such assignments, which are chiefly involved with running the prison itself rather than tasks that might be useful after release. The government has also allowed some private businesses to employ prison labor, but the costs and requirements, along with union opposition, are so difficult that few firms have done so.

One step beyond prison is work release programs, where convicts work at jobs outside the walls for brief periods. However, such a program in Washington State in the early 1990s failed to cut recidivism or save money; rather, like intensive parole, it generated more technical violations and returns to prison. A further step is guaranteed jobs for ex-offenders after they have left prison. Ex-offenders were one of the groups served in the National Supported Work Demonstration of the late 1970s, but they showed negligible gains in work and none in recidivism.[23]

Nonetheless, work programs reduce crime more among older men than younger men. These men may have aged beyond some of the debilitating drive for respect mentioned in chapter 2. They are readier to accept working in jobs that are mostly low skilled and low paid.[24]

Local Programs. Of recent work programs aimed at ex-offenders, the most prominent is Texas's Project RIO (Re-Integration of Offenders). With more than seventy thousand prison releases a year, this giant state accounts for nearly a tenth of national releases all by itself.[25] RIO began in Dallas and Houston in 1985 and went statewide in 1993. It prepares ex-offenders for employment through education and training in prison and then on their release works to place them quickly in jobs. Outside the prisons, RIO resembles NCP Choices. Run largely by the Texas Workforce Commission (TWC), it provides staff to serve a disadvantaged group that otherwise could not compete for attention with TWC's more employable walk-in clientele.[26]

RIO is a large program. Outside the prisons, it has more than one hundred staff in sixty-two offices around the state. According to a federal study, in 1995 RIO served 15,366 parolees, representing about 40 percent of all ex-offenders (and 47 percent of all parolees) released from prison that year. It has placed in jobs 69 percent of the more than 100,000 ex-offenders it has served since 1985, including 74 percent of the clients served in 1995. With better enforcement, it could be larger still. Typically, only 10 to 55 percent of referrals to the program show up, and little pressure is put on them to attend as long as they do not violate parole.[27]

ComALERT is a prison reentry program focused mainly on drug treatment in Brooklyn, New York. The King's County (Brooklyn) district attorney's office began the program in 2001 in collaboration with a local drug treatment and counseling nongovernmental organization and the Doe Fund, which runs transitional employment and housing programs for homeless men. Parole officers refer ex-offenders to ComALERT as they come out of prison with substance abuse problems. These parolees must participate in counseling and drug treatment. To graduate, they must be drug free for three months and employed or in school. They are then referred on to other services as needed.

In addition, clients may volunteer for the Doe Fund's Ready, Willing, and Able program. This program requires participants to work in community service positions while participating in twelve-step programs, receiving other training, and, if needed, living in supported housing. Clients are regularly tested for drug use and dismissed if they test positive. After nine months, they transition to paid employment and regular housing and graduate from the program.[28]

America Works also runs a prison reentry program in New York City, but with quite a different approach. The Criminal Justice program receives mandatory referrals of ex-offenders on parole from New York State prisons. Modeled on America Works's welfare work approach, the program runs clients through brief orientation and job-readiness training and then places them with private employers who have been recruited by America Works's sales force. If men fail at the first job, they are placed again, until retention improves. Once placed, they are visited by staff to work out problems that may impede retention.[29]

Center for Employment Opportunities. The Center for Employment Opportunities (CEO), also in New York City, is the most important reentry program to date. Similar to PFS in child support, it is the only program of its type with a completed experimental evaluation.[30] It is also conspicuously successful. Although still evolving, it already conveys important lessons about how poor men might be put to work.

Located in downtown Manhattan, CEO receives most of its referrals from local parole officers, although some come directly from New York State prisons. It also serves some youth exiting jails in New York City. It gives new clients a week of orientation to the workplace and then assigns them to transitional jobs doing cleaning and repairs at government buildings around

New York City. CEO maintains approximately thirty-five work crews of five to nine men each for this purpose. Supervisors rate the men's attendance, comportment, and other qualities daily, and the men are paid daily at the local minimum wage, currently $7.25 an hour. These positions may last up to seventy-five days.

Once established in their work, clients meet with "job coaches" who help them with other problems, such as health, housing, or ties to families. After two weeks of work, they also see a job developer, who seeks to place them in unsubsidized, full-time positions. About 60 percent of clients are placed within three months. After the men are placed, staff follow up with them on the job for up to a year, seeking to sort out problems and promote job retention.

CEO has several features suggested by past research and experience with men's work programs. It emphasizes immediate immersion in paid employment and deemphasizes the training and ancillary services that PFS provided. It is paternalistic and prescriptive. Men receive constant supervision, and constructive attitudes and behavior are strongly promoted.

CEO has placed about ten thousand people in unsubsidized employment since its founding in 1996. It currently serves about two thousand clients a year. However, this is a small share of the twenty-five thousand ex-offenders returning from New York State prisons annually.[31]

Transitional Jobs Reentry Demonstration. CEO resembles the Transitional Jobs Reentry Demonstration (TJRD) that the Joyce Foundation is running at four sites in the Midwest.[32] Here, too, ex-offenders are assigned to temporary jobs arranged by the program and then placed in unsubsidized jobs largely in the private sector. But unlike CEO, the jobs in most cases are provided by community organizations serving various groups with employment problems, not only ex-offenders.

Service-Oriented Programs

The above programs are all in some sense mandatory. Ex-offenders are referred to them by the prison or parole systems, although how strictly attendance is enforced varies. Some other reentry programs have been more service oriented and participation is voluntary. These are the equivalent of the fatherhood programs considered in chapter 3. They embody a more indulgent, barriers-oriented view of the causes of men's work problems. The goals were more to involve faith-based initiatives in serving ex-offenders than to enforce work.[33]

Ready4Work was a demonstration program run at seventeen sites during 2003–2006 with $25 million in funding from the U.S. Departments of Justice and Labor and private foundations. Services were provided by a consortium of agencies, headed in most cases by a faith-based organization. The clients were nonviolent ex-offenders aged eighteen to thirty-four and mostly black. For up to a year, they received various employment services and met with mentors either individually or in groups.

The Serious and Violent Offenders Reentry Initiative (SVORI) was a major $110 million research effort of the National Institute of Justice launched in 2003. Sixty-nine state agencies received grants of $500,000 to $2 million over three years to develop eighty-nine reentry programs. The main goal was to expand services for ex-offenders and promote collaboration among agencies at the federal and local levels. Whereas some reentry efforts exclude violent offenders, SVORI focuses on them. Programs vary, with most stressing employment. Like the fatherhood initiatives, many of these programs have had difficulty enrolling clients; 60 percent of programs have one hundred or fewer participants.[34]

The President's Prisoner Reentry Initiative was an extension of Ready4Work launched by President George W. Bush and, like Ready4Work, run by the U.S. Department of Labor. It aimed to enlist faith-based and community organizations in helping returning prisoners. Funding of $20 million a year began in 2005 and was scheduled to last four years, conditional on appropriations. Clients were mentored, and education and training services were to be provided via vouchers by private organizations. This program has not yet generated evaluation results.

Evaluations

As with the child support programs, the evaluations of the prison reentry programs are limited. Yet the evidence suggests that well-designed programs, if well implemented, can probably raise work levels and reduce recidivism among ex-prisoners.

Center for Employment Opportunities. CEO's results are the most important because they are experimental and also positive. Over the three years since the experiment began, the program has demonstrated the following:

- *Large but mostly transient impacts on employment:* In the first year, 80 percent of experimental clients worked, a gain of 24 percentage points or 43 percent over the controls, largely due to the transitional jobs. However, this effect fell over the year to the point where it was no longer statistically significant in the last quarter. This decline reflects the men's moving into private-sector jobs, where they were less closely supervised and their retention fell.

- *Reductions in recidivism:* Over three years, experimental clients were almost 6 percentage points or 11 percent less likely to be convicted of a new crime. Several other measures of recidivism also showed significant improvements. Such a clear and sustained impact on recidivism has been extremely rare in criminal justice programming.

- *Impacts varied by subgroup:* Effects were generally stronger for ex-offenders who enrolled in CEO within three months of leaving prison than for those who enrolled later. Three-year recidivism impacts were entirely concentrated among the early enrollees and for this group ran as high as 9 points or 62 percent. The program also showed a small impact on private employment for this group late in the three-year follow-up period, although there were no impacts on earnings. These results corroborate the views of experts that reentry services should involve men quickly upon their release.

- *Savings for taxpayers:* Although CEO cost $3,600 more per client than the services received by the control group, it saved about $3,800 per client because of its impacts on recidivism. If benefits to victims and clients' employment are considered, the net benefit rises to $4,600 per client. For the recently released subgroup, the net benefit was $7,500 with victim benefits, including $4,500 in criminal justice savings.[35]

CEO has achieved such results even though it is still a work in progress. Its large employment impact is notable, given the importance of raising men's work levels. It suggests the effects that a combination of assuring and enforcing work might have. The rapid decline of the effect clearly reflects the difficulty the men have transitioning from the program's own jobs to the private sector. To improve its retention in private placement, CEO created a retention unit to follow up with clients on the job and address problems there. It also has instituted Rapid Rewards, a bonus of up to $200 a year that ex-offenders receive for achieving certain milestones in job retention. The program claims to have improved its job retention rate at 180 days after placement from 40 to 60 percent.[36]

Transitional Jobs Reentry Demonstration. The evaluation of TJRD recorded first-year results much like those for CEO. There were strong impacts on employment and earnings, but these were entirely due to the transitional jobs. There were no impacts on unsubsidized employment, and no overall impact on employment after a year. Unlike CEO, the program showed virtually no impacts on recidivism. If TJRD does less well than CEO, the reason is probably that it is less intensive. The transitional jobs are provided by community organizations that are less focused on ex-offenders than CEO, and they also involve higher numbers of workers per supervisor. The supervisors do not oversee performance as closely as CEO's crew chiefs, who rate workers daily on many criteria. It is also likely that private jobs placement after the transitional jobs is less well developed than at CEO.[37]

TJRD still expresses an idea that what ex-offenders most need to work is improved opportunities. Although CEO also offers jobs, it primarily reflects the realization that the key to employment is improved work discipline. Of the two programs, TJRD is conceived more in economic terms, CEO in more institutional ones, and the latter approach achieves more.

Local Programs. Project RIO received an evaluation based on statistical matching performed at Texas A&M University in 1992. After one year of follow-up, 69 percent of program participants had found work, compared to 36 percent of parolees not in the program. During that year, RIO clients worked during 1.8 quarters on average, compared to 1.1 quarters for non-RIO ex-offenders. Researchers estimated that nearly 20 percent of those served avoided recidivism through the program. These impacts might be overstated because the matching of program and comparison clients was imprecise due to limited data sources. However, the apparent effect is large enough to be encouraging.[38]

ComALERT received a careful evaluation based on propensity score matching. Results showed that over two years the following occurred:

- *Employment improved.* Government data suggest that clients in the program worked more and had higher earnings than comparison clients. In a survey, the employment gains appeared much greater—three or four times. Much of the gain was attributable, as in CEO, to the men's working in transitional jobs arranged by the program—the Doe Fund's Ready, Willing, and Able program.

- *Recidivism was reduced.* ComALERT clients as a whole were about 15 percent less likely to be rearrested, reconvicted, and reincarcerated than the comparison group, and the difference was twice that for the subset of clients who successfully graduated from the program.

- *Substance abuse fell.* There was weaker evidence that drug and alcohol abuse fell among program clients relative to controls.

- *Family effects were nil.* As in PFS, there was no evidence that program clients were more likely to reside with partners or have more contact with their children.

- *Effects varied.* Clients who graduated from ComALERT showed stronger impacts than those who merely participated. That might be because the program had more chance to influence them, or it might reflect selection effects.

Like CEO, ComALERT is a work in progress. The tested program was oriented mainly to drug treatment, but its strongest results were for clients who also volunteered for Ready, Willing, and Able. That suggests that the program needs to improve its employment services, as it is now doing. To maximize impacts, work may have to be required and guaranteed to all clients, as in CEO.[39]

America Works is currently receiving an experimental evaluation by Public/Private Ventures, but the study has not yet returned results.

Service-Oriented Programs. Ready4Work reported only outcomes, with no counterfactual, from its eleven sites serving adult offenders. Results showed that 56 percent of participants held a job for at least a month while in the program, and 60 percent of those who found jobs kept them for at least three months, a third for at least six months. Furthermore, only 3 percent of participants returned to prison for a new offense within six months of their release, compared to 5 percent for a national sample of returnees; only 7 percent did so within a year, compared to 10 percent nationally. For black, nonviolent offenders, recidivism ran more than 40 percent below national norms. Some of those apparent gains might have been due to the mentoring provided by the program.[40]

SVORI has impact estimates for several outcomes based on propensity score matching. These suggest that the program successfully increased the services received by its clients, but gains in outcomes compared to men not in the program were generally small, around 5 to 15 percent. Ex-offenders in the program were about 10 percent more likely to be working three months after leaving prison than were comparison clients not in the program. Their jobs were more likely to be permanent, to offer formal pay, and to include benefits.[41]

Conclusion

In criminal reentry, as in child support enforcement, we see the emergence of new work programs for low-skilled men. And like child support, the criminal justice system has begun reaching out to a broader community. Prisons and parole officers look beyond themselves for services they have not provided and also for some of the supervision that ex-offenders appear to need.

The development of men's programs is somewhat more limited in criminal justice than in child support. That is probably because law enforcement is less willing to change and also because ex-offenders arouse more fear than men who merely fail to pay child support. The public may be more reluctant to help them, especially if parolees commit new and visible crimes.

On the other hand, there may be less disagreement about how to serve these men than there is in child support. The division between programs oriented to enforcing work and those oriented to services appears less pronounced. There is no political battle comparable to the struggle between feminist and fathers' rights groups in child support. There is more acceptance, even among liberals, that an element of authority is essential to moving these men toward regular employment.

5

Implementing Programs

The previous two chapters established that men's work programs aimed at child support defaulters and ex-offenders probably could raise their work levels *if* well implemented. But what would it take to establish such programs on a wide scale? My own research concentrated largely on this question. In this chapter, after a brief discussion of previous implementation research, I suggest in general terms what expanding work programs would require. I then look in more depth at the implementation problems already faced by the child support and criminal justice systems and what taking on work programs would mean. Later chapters will describe what states have actually done.

Past Research

Most previous research about men's work problems concerns the men themselves or the programs that do or do not help them. There is very little about the institutional setting—the political and administrative factors that determine whether and how such programs are instituted. This largely reflects the dominance of policy research by economists rather than political scientists and also the lack of easily available data on the institutions.

Even to perceive the institutions, one must leave one's computer, venture out into the field, and interview local and state officials. That sort of research commands less prestige in academe than statistical modeling, but it reveals more about the nature of change. Welfare reform was achieved largely by politicians and administrators at the state and local levels. A lack of research at this level was one reason why the potential for reform was underestimated and why most welfare experts opposed it.[1]

In welfare reform, however, we could at least examine several case studies of change at the state level.[2] On that basis, we could generalize about the factors favoring strong or weak implementation of TANF.[3] For men's programs, there is nothing comparable. Of the program evaluations considered earlier, only PFS's included a thorough analysis of the institutional setting and the challenges this posed.[4] I have relied on that work heavily. Implementation research on the fatherhood programs describes difficulties in setting up the programs, especially their recruitment problems, but with less context and background.[5] I know of no research on the implementation of prison reentry programs, in part because they are more recent.

Getting to Scale

What stands out about the men's programs we have reviewed is that most are *small*, *voluntary*, and *detached*. With the exception of NCP Choices and Project RIO in Texas, all are small both absolutely and relative to their potential caseload. Not all programs enforced participation, and even the mandatory programs did so only selectively. Again, with the possible exception of the Texas programs, no program was central to regular child support or criminal justice operations. Most were demonstrations with special funding that left the regular institutions unchanged.

These features are interconnected. The programs are small in part because they are voluntary, and they are voluntary in part because they are detached from mainstream institutions with the power to enforce. To have more impact, they would have to grow. To do that they would have to become mandatory and enforce participation. For nonworking men, entry into a work program would have to become usual, not unusual. And for this to happen, work programs would have to be built into regular child support and the criminal justice operations.

The key to enforcement is that the penalty be immediate and reliable, not that it be severe. If the authorities sanction people for noncompliance with social norms but without close tie to the offenses, they will have little effect. Disorder will reign, even if many people are penalized. Conversely, if offenders know they face certain and immediate consequences, they will tend to comply. Order will then be achieved even if very few people are penalized. All depends on whether enforcement is credible "on the ground."[6]

The Welfare Precedent. In the 1980s, efforts to move welfare mothers into jobs had all the features that men's work programs have today. They too were small, largely voluntary, service oriented, and peripheral to the mainstream institutions, which in this case meant welfare. Although work programs linked to welfare existed and were in theory mandatory, welfare departments largely ignored them. The programs had virtually no effect on welfare mothers, who remained largely nonworking. Some private efforts to serve poor mothers were also made, parallel to the service-oriented men's programs, but they too had little impact because they had no authority to get their clients to change their lives.[7] Some programs placed welfare mothers in unpaid jobs, the most literal form of work test, but they remained small, usually involving only a few of the many mothers who failed to work.[8]

Only when work programs became more directive, in the late 1980s and 1990s, were they able to grow, get the attention of their intended clients, and motivate change. They grew because work requirements were strengthened and, above all, because the welfare system took on employment as a central mission. In many states, mothers seeking cash aid were told first to look for a job. Only after that could they get assistance. Work programs grew much bigger than before, although "workfare"—the literal working off of grants in government jobs—remained uncommon.

Eventually, work demands became so clear that many poor mothers never went on welfare at all, but directly to work. Those "diversion" effects occurred off caseload, but they were the most fundamental change that welfare reform achieved. Reform now reached beyond welfare itself to change the surrounding society. It was now expected that poor mothers would go to work before seeking aid, and aid itself would be premised on work effort. Without this shift, reform could not have produced the revolution it did.[9]

Such changes did not occur overnight. As long as the welfare rolls were large, it was difficult to enforce work because of the sheer numbers. Dependency in this sense fed on itself. In response, it took a massive administrative buildup over years to get on top of this caseload, to make the work demand serious "on the ground," at the local level where recipients encounter welfare. Growing pressure to work generated diversion. But once that happened, welfare shrunk, and it became progressively easier to require work of the remaining cases. Finally, enforcement could shrink along with the rolls while still maintaining the work norm in the surrounding society. Today, welfare has to enforce work explicitly on only the small share of poor mothers who remain on the rolls. In a similar way, to maintain the norm of tax payments, the Internal Revenue Service needs to audit only a small proportion of tax returns.

How Much Is Enough? For low-skilled men, steady work is currently rare because it is unenforced, as it once was for welfare mothers. The sheer scale of the work problem defeats enforcement. But if work programs were implemented seriously for the groups I have identified—low-income child support defaulters and parolees—that would motivate higher work effort for all low-income men, not only those explicitly subject to the requirements. To achieve this, government must once again get on top of a caseload. It must raise the share of men with a work obligation who actually *have* to work. More and more of them must be located and inducted into work programs until the obligation to work becomes real and immediate, not just a distant goal. Then voluntary work levels should rise—the male form of diversion effects. Then explicit enforcement could be scaled back, as it has been in welfare.

How far implementation must go to achieve these effects is unclear. In welfare even today, only around a third of TANF cases actually participate in work activities. Yet, coupled with the new benefits and available jobs, that has been enough to drive most welfare mothers off the rolls, mostly into work. In the cost estimates below, I have assumed that men's work programs would have to serve all poor men who have both work obligations and work problems, but in practice to serve fewer than that might be enough to generate a work message and raise work levels. On the other hand, to enforce work for this group would not address the work problems of the mainstream unemployed and other men with a steadier job history. Few of them are obligated to work now because few are nonpayers of child support or ex-offenders on parole.

In part, men's work programs are small because they are positioned well back in the administrative process. In welfare, too, work programs were once confined to mothers who had persistently failed to work. There was thought to be a tradeoff between serving the bulk of the caseload superficially and serving a smaller, more disadvantaged share more intensively. Many experts thought it was better to wait for the bulk of mothers to leave aid voluntarily and then concentrate work services on the hard-core cases.[10] But this approach did not communicate a strong work message. It still treated employment as a benefit to be provided to some mothers, not an obligation incumbent on all of them. As reform escalated in the 1990s, states moved toward demanding work from mothers up front, as soon as they went on aid, often even before their applications were approved. That sent a much stronger work message, and it was this that generated the diversion effects of the later 1990s.

Likewise, in men's programs, current clients tend to be the more disadvantaged men who have persistently failed to work or pay child support on their own. All others have been penalized or excused on various grounds earlier in the process. So the numbers served are much smaller than the numbers who are out of compliance. In NCP Choices, for example, the only men assigned are those whose families are or have been on welfare (because the program is funded through TANF). They also must owe at least $5,000 in arrears, be in dispute with CSE, live in an area served by NCP Choices, and also not be on disability benefits (or have applied for them).

If they are conceived this narrowly, the programs are unlikely to generate any general change in expectations about work. Large as it is, NCP Choices is probably too small to generate diversion effects, at least in a state as large as Texas. A serious men's work strategy must reach a higher share of nonworking men so that the work obligation they already bear becomes credible "on the ground."

The Implementation Problem

What, in general, would it take to institute larger and more demanding programs? This question touches on the well-known challenges of implementing social programs. Typically, these programs are conducted by local agencies on behalf of national or state governments, who fund them subject to conditions. The Great Society programs of the 1960s and 1970s gained a reputation for ineffectiveness, but much of this was because they were not carried out as designed. The programs were planned largely by economists who conceived them in terms of the benefits or incentives they generated. Later the programs would be evaluated. But planners typically ignored the linkages that lay between laws passed by Congress or state legislatures and the eventual social effects.[11] In recent decades, programmatic chains of command have become even more complex, with the frequent use of private and nonprofit contractors to deliver services.[12] The child support and criminal justice programs we have discussed already show that tendency.

Some political scientists concluded that higher-level authorities could have only limited control over the programs they fund. Trying to manage programs through grants to lower-level agencies was like pushing a string. Whatever the grantors intended, local operators would inevitably twist programs to serve their own priorities, if they implemented them at all. Others argued that superiors could force through new policies if the legal mandate were strong enough and the funding was sufficient.[13] In welfare reform, the goal of raising work levels was widely shared, reducing conflict. Governments at all levels competed to achieve work, and this was one reason TANF was generally well implemented.[14]

A fair consensus of the implementation literature is that implementation of a program will vary *positively with political will and funding,* that is, success requires that the authorities behind the program agree about a problem and its solution, accept that solving it is important, and provide the necessary resources. But implementation will vary *negatively with bureaucratic complexity.* The more agencies and governmental levels involved in running a program, the more troubled its implementation will be. Complexity raises the chance of conflicting goals.[15]

If we now examine the chief arenas of men's program development, we find many conditions adverse to implementation. Both child support enforcement and criminal justice already face difficult tasks. To ask them, in addition, to get more clients to work will require major changes in goals and routines.

Child Support Enforcement

The original mission of child support enforcement was to get absent parents to pay support to their families. To do that requires locating absent fathers, determining their paternity, setting support orders, and then enforcing them. As noted in chapter 3, the system has made progress on all these fronts, but getting low-income fathers to pay remains unsolved. It was to address that problem that work programs in child support first arose.

Goals. Despite this problem with low-income fathers, child support has not traditionally focused on employment. Officials know that most fathers have to have earnings in order to pay their judgments, yet child support's main routines have assumed work rather than helping men achieve it. This assumption appears to reflect the system's origins in the civil law system that dealt chiefly with the middle class. The father was usually employed, so the problem was ordinarily to get him to pay, not to get him to work. Thus, CSE inherited the idea that its challenge was the "deadbeat dad"—one who could pay his judgment but wouldn't.[16] As one local child support lawyer said to me, "It's all about the money."

Thus, CSE tended to focus on fathers who were able to pay, not the non-workers who could not. Even if the latter could be found and their wages garnished, they had little income to contribute. So these cases tended not to be "worked" regularly. The pressure to make money from enforcement has only increased in recent decades as the system has run in the red (see below) and federal incentives have focused on the efficient use of funds.[17]

Not working is at the center of poor men's problems. To raise these men's work levels would generate many benefits beyond just more child support. But CSE never focused on getting men to work as an end in itself. Welfare adopted the goal of employing welfare mothers in the 1980s and 1990s because it was good for families, not just because it would reduce dependency. CSE has not made a comparable shift. As several CSE officials said to me, "We're not social workers."

To be sure, CSE has become more father friendly in recent years. Many officials now accept that it is not constructive just to crack down on poor fathers.[18] That is one reason work programs have developed. But the tendency still is to keep the pressure on the men to pay, even if this may keep some from working at all. CSE may refuse to adjust an order downward (reduce the amount expected) when a father is jobless, for example, lest it create a disincentive to work.[19] The idea that getting the men employed might actually be more important than getting them to pay is still radical.

The fatherhood programs have somewhat different goals. On the one hand, they might be seen as resources for child support, as they help fathers come to terms with the demands of that system. On the other hand, they arose in part in opposition to child support, or at least to the severity of its demands. And although they promote work by fathers, these programs do not focus on enforcement. Their emphasis is more on reaching out to fathers and helping them come to terms with their families and their lives. It is thus doubtful that these programs can help CSE raise work levels.

Administration. Another obstacle to change in child support is the complexity of the system. Typically, at the state level there is a CSE agency with responsibility for identifying noncustodial fathers who should be paying support. It takes the lead in locating the men and establishing paternity and support orders. But the final decisions on paternity and orders usually rest with local child support judges. Once finalized, the order is relayed to a separate payment administration, usually at the state level, that garnishes the father's wages and distributes the proceeds to the family and (if welfare or Medicaid is involved) to the state and federal governments. If the father then fails to pay or disappears, the case is referred back to CSE, which goes back to the judge for enforcement actions. Sometimes follow-up rests with a different body—in Michigan, local agencies known as Friend of the Court.

Judges complicate enforcement, although they are also a source of authority. Traditionally, in setting support orders, child support judges were arbitrary and uneven and often lenient. This offended the groups who wanted fathers to pay more to support families. The main reason Congress forced states to impose uniform payment scales on the judges in the 1980s was to make them more consistent and demanding. Since then, the federal government has urged states to reduce the judges' role and give more discretion to CSE administrators, and some have done so. This shift has allowed orders to be set and updated more quickly as men's jobs or earnings change. It may also allow quicker reaction to noncompliance. However, judges remain central to the system. A good part of implementing child support work programs is getting the judges to refer men to them and then enforce their attendance.

In addition to all this, work programs require further effort to place men in jobs and keep them there. To accomplish this, child support has typically looked to the workforce system—the voluntary training agencies currently financed under the Workforce Investment Act (WIA). It is not enough simply to refer nonpayers there; they would have to compete with the walk-in clientele, who are typically more attractive to the agencies and employers. Special workforce staff must be funded to serve the defaulters, as in Texas's NCP Choices. Other possibilities include using welfare work programs.

One difficulty with the workforce system is that traditionally it did not enforce work. Its routines assume that clients are willing workers who seek out its services on their own. That assumption goes back to the Employment Service, or Job Service, the oldest part of the workforce system, a federally funded labor exchange that dates from the 1930s. The same assumption was made by federal training programs first set up in the 1960s and now funded under WIA. Thus, the workforce system does not normally provide services to overcome work inhibitions or invoke authority to require work. In ethos, it is the opposite of CSE. Whereas CSE stresses enforcement but traditionally ignores employment, workforce stresses employment and training but ignores enforcement. Without a WIA structure willing and able to enforce work, CSE has trouble running work programs at all.

When welfare work programs first arose in the 1960s and 1970s, they were run by the Employment Service, and that was one reason they were ineffective. Only in the 1980s did states obtain authority to shift the work mission elsewhere. In Wisconsin and other pioneer states, the welfare department set up its own work operation, which was more insistent about enforcing work than the Employment Service. However, in the 1990s, many states again vested the welfare work mission in the workforce system, leading to serious implementation problems. Welfare clients were often not referred to the workforce smoothly, nor was their attendance there monitored and enforced.[20]

However, some workforce agencies have come around to accept work enforcement. Adopting this role, they have learned, is one way they can earn financial support. The conversion of WIA in Texas to that role was crucial to that state's successes in men's programming, as I note below.

Financing. Child support also has trouble funding work programs. For years, CSE made money for government by using child support collections to recoup some of the cost of welfare for families abandoned by fathers. But since the dramatic decline in the welfare rolls in the 1990s, that offset has shriveled. And while CSE was created initially to battle dependency, it has since the 1980s come to serve most child support cases both on and off welfare. Table 3-1 shows that the share of child support collections made under Title IV-D rose from only 23 percent in 1978 to 93 percent in 2005. Most collections now go to families—not government. Thus, the system has lost money for the federal government since 1980 and for government overall since 1990. In 2006, its net cost was over $3 billion.[21]

To implement work programs in child support, therefore, both the child support and workforce systems must change their cultures and routines. An already complicated network of agencies must become still more complex, yet focused on a new mission—employment. Making this change will require leadership from OCSE, backed up by the leading states that have already begun to make the change. And new resources will be necessary. Localities cannot routinely afford to run work programs in child support unless dedicated funding is provided, as it was, for example, through the Welfare-to-Work grants of the late 1990s. Expanding work programs on a permanent basis could require a regular federal funding stream, akin to those that support WIA or TANF.

Criminal Justice

For the criminal justice system to implement work programs on a large scale would also require major reorientations in both purpose and organization. There is also less willingness to change than in child support.

Goals. State prison and parole systems seek chiefly to enforce the law and punish lawbreakers. Punishment may be seen as protecting society from offenders and deterring future crime, and also as a means of rehabilitating the offender or expressing society's disapproval of crime. But of all these purposes, only rehabilitation has any close connection to employment. The system also resists assuming responsibility for employment because it insists that convicts accept responsibility for crime and recovery. For government to do much to help them work violates that premise.

Hard-line attitudes toward offenders have also been fostered in recent decades by the perceived failure of alternatives to incarceration. If we cannot rehabilitate and if parole has little effect, then public safety is served only by keeping men behind bars. To that mindset, the very idea of releasing men to work programs is suspect. Even officials who still believe in rehabilitation will doubt that work has any special power to overcome criminogenic attitudes. The reentry approach involves some shift of goals toward greater concern for the men leaving prison, although the claim is that public safety will also be served. Advocates of reentry, therefore, have to demonstrate that helping men reenter society does not mean going soft on them.

Structure. The criminal justice system is more complicated than may first appear. In many states, probation is an arm of the criminal courts. The prisons and parole are separate. Although all these systems may be under one umbrella department in some states, in others they are entirely separate.

Judges, as in child support, play an important role. Specialized courts such as "drug courts" have developed in some states where judges intensively oversee particular types of cases. Offenders in rehabilitation appear before the same judge repeatedly to review their progress and confront relapses. Some—such as Judge Kristin Ruth of North Carolina—have used and advocated this same approach for chronic child support defaulters. Jeremy Travis has proposed "reentry courts" that would oversee parole as adjuncts of parole officers.[22]

The reentry model introduces further players from outside the traditional criminal justice system. Community groups and nonprofit organizations would enter the prisons to prepare offenders for release and then provide them with services afterward. Interacting with these bodies is a sharp change for the public agencies, which have usually been largely autonomous.

As mentioned earlier, a further challenge is that parole's authority over ex-offenders has weakened as fewer men leave prison subject to supervision. For these cases, child support may actually offer a way to enforce work where the criminal justice system no longer can.

As in child support, national leadership can help to promote the work goal for criminal justice. However, the federal role in law enforcement is more limited than in child support. There is no major federal funding stream.

Past Programs

The programs we have examined suggest that implementing work programs for men is indeed challenging. The task requires creating a new institution to serve nonpaying, nonworking men within systems that usually give work little priority.

That process is best documented in the case of PFS. Here the creators of the experimental program had to persuade child support agencies, accustomed to getting all they could from fathers, to reduce demands on them as long as they participated in the experiment. The program worked best in the localities where CSE was strongly committed to it and where staff combined their helping and enforcing roles best. PFS also had to persuade training programs to place noncustodial fathers in desirable training slots such as on-the-job training even though these men seemed less qualified than other candidates. Finally, the program had to persuade the men themselves to face their problems and the child support system, which many were unused to doing. Against all these challenges it had only limited success.[23]

The fatherhood programs operated with less reliance on the mainline agencies than the enforcement programs, yet they could not avoid them. Their clients had to learn about child support and meet its demands if they were to avert serious trouble. Many men showed little interest in training because of a desire to earn immediate money to meet their obligations. Yet some had to complete their educations, and others needed access to training, so the programs had to engage with the school and workforce systems.

We know less about how prison reentry programs were established. CEO and ComALERT were created by inspired entrepreneurs at the local level. Although these programs appear to succeed, they are exemplars rather than forces for systemic change. The work of building employment into criminal justice more broadly has only just begun.

6

The State Survey

This research included a survey of all the states to find out how many had implemented work programs in either child support or criminal justice. Despite the difficulties mentioned in the last chapter, we found that states have begun to institute work programs for men on a substantial scale.[1]

The survey was conservatively framed to identify only work programs intended for child support defaulters or ex-offenders. Also, the programs had to be *in addition to* those that the states already used to promote work among low-income adults, such as the workforce system or TANF work programs. A program meant more than just having regular child support or parole staff refer men elsewhere for services. There had to be a distinct staff that the state was spending money on for the purpose of raising *these* men's work levels, even if all it did was refer men to other agencies. Furthermore, the programs had to be state run, even if they were not statewide. This requirement excluded purely local programs, of which there were many. We also counted only programs running at the time we talked to a state in 2009, excluding programs that had ended or were to begin in the future.

Our questions aimed at basic description. Did a state have work programs in child support or criminal justice? If so in either area, which agency ran it and how was it funded? Was it mandatory in the sense that men had to participate on pain of some penalty? How large was the caseload relative to all men who might be subject to it? And what services did it offer, including referral to other programs, job search, guaranteed jobs, or training?

In the phone survey, we found it difficult to locate officials willing and able to talk. We had to call some states repeatedly. On both the child support and criminal justice sides, forty-three out of fifty-one jurisdictions finally responded. Nevertheless, we are confident that our results are representative. For more detail on the survey, see the appendix.

Findings

In child support, 47 percent of responding states had work programs. Ninety percent of these programs were mandatory. Nearly all the programs offered a range of services, including referral to other programs, job search, and training. Yet respondents made clear that they were oriented strongly to work first—placing men in available jobs. None attempted to guarantee jobs.

In criminal justice, work programs were even more common, occurring in 65 percent of responding states. Only a quarter of these programs were mandatory, involving an enforceable referral. Parole officers did not usually *require* that their clients enter a work program, yet the overall structure was still mandatory because parolees in most states are required to work as a condition of parole. As in child support, the programs nearly all provided referral, job search, and training in some form, yet the overall focus was strongly on work first. In this area, three out of twenty-eight programs, or 11 percent, did claim to guarantee jobs.

In child support, 60 percent of the work programs were funded and run by child support itself, most of the rest by TANF or the workforce system. Some programs had federal grants (for example, OCSE, Social Security Act section 1115, or Department of Labor). Some served a wide range of non-payers, but others were limited to cases with a welfare connection because funding came from TANF.

In criminal justice, likewise, three-quarters of the programs were funded and run by criminal justice itself and the rest mostly by the workforce system. Some also drew grants from the U.S. Departments of Justice or Labor, the president's reentry initiative, or the Serious and Violent Offenders Reentry Initiative. These programs also differed in the extent of supervision given to clients. Some states had very cursory parole operations, whereas others were strict. Some programs simply referred men to the regular workforce system, whereas others provided special case managers for employment. Programs tended to be narrowly focused and small, in part because many were residential and had limited beds. Child support could cast a wider net because their men were on average less disadvantaged.

Although the programs were widespread, they were typically small, like the programs discussed above. In child support, three-quarters of respondents said the programs served only a small minority of the clients who might have been assigned to them, 15 percent said a large minority, and 10 percent a large majority. On the criminal justice side, 36 percent said they served a small minority, 32 percent a large minority, and 32 percent a large or small majority.

Trends over Time

A survey conducted at one point in time cannot document trends, but conversations with respondents made clear that the movement toward men's work programs was fairly recent. No current program appears to be older than Texas's Project RIO, begun in 1985. Respondents, especially in child support, spoke of a growing realization of the need to raise men's work levels. Had we surveyed states ten or twenty years ago, there would likely have been far less activity.

But expansion has not been smooth. Many programs were being started up, others closed down. The immediate reason for closings was usually budget cuts due to the recession. Most of the federal funding was project based and thus time limited. In other cases, including Michigan and Ohio, child support funding based on TANF had fallen. In still other states, programs came to be seen as ineffective. Few states had found a relatively stable program structure, as in Texas.

To expand programs more permanently would mean solving the implementation problems already mentioned. Men's work programs would need steadier sources of funding that could be counted on year after year, like TANF or the workforce system. A buildup would also require more case managers to oversee clients. Programs must also be dovetailed with the existing child support, parole, and workforce systems. The greatest need would be for political commitment. In welfare reform, pioneers like Wisconsin did not realize all that reform involved at the outset. They had to solve problems as they emerged. Nevertheless, they were committed to change, so they persevered until welfare was transformed.

The same is true with men's work programs. The survey suggested that some states are edging up to the starting line of serious action, but few have crossed it. The next chapter explores in more depth what committed implementation would require.

7

Field Interviews

Field interviews in six diverse states during 2008–2009 allowed me to explore in more depth how political and administrative factors shaped the emergence of work programs. The states I visited included some where I had contacts and could get entrée (New Jersey, New York, and Wisconsin) and others where I had heard of important developments in men's programming (Michigan, Ohio, and Texas). I also chose the states to be broadly representative of the nation.

I interviewed child support and criminal justice officials at the state level and in at least one locality in each state. I aimed at people involved in decisions about work programs in the state or in implementing them locally. Thus I chiefly met with public officials, although in some cases my respondents were from private agencies that had been contracted to implement programs. I did not interview anyone in the fatherhood programs because these programs seemed largely detached from the work-implementation problem, and my agency respondents virtually never mentioned them. For more detail about my interviews, see the appendix.

I emphasize that I am not rating the states as more or less successful. Those with the most dramatic initiatives, such as Michigan and Texas, are the most interesting if one thinks men's programs have potential, but local conditions differ, and it is too early to say that all states must go down this road.

Below, I summarize how my respondents saw the men's work problem and describe what each of the six states was doing about it at the time of my visits in late 2008 and early 2009. I propose an analytic scheme, based on welfare reform, to explain which states were more or less ambitious in men's programming. My findings largely confirm these expectations.

The View from the Field

The state survey could not elicit the view of officials in any depth, but amid describing their programs, state officials also indicated that they largely agreed with the interpretation of the men's work problem and its causes offered in chapters 1 and 2. Most spoke of "barriers" to work, but they located these more in the personal lives of the clients than in the economy, and most believed that some element of enforcement as well as new programs were essential to get men to work more regularly.

In the fieldwork states, I was able to probe opinions more fully. I asked respondents what the "men's work problem" connoted to them and how they would explain it. Almost all characterized it as a combination of irregular work and work at low wages. The men they dealt with never became "established" in the workforce and thus could seldom get "family sustaining" jobs. As to causes, most respondents spoke of "barriers" that kept men from working regularly, but again they located these largely in the men's personal lives. They cited lack of education, skills, training, and, above all, a lack of "structure" in the men's past lives. Many of these men lacked the elemental discipline, such as showing up to the job on time and taking orders, needed to succeed at work. Many simply had never been workers and had no idea what that involved.

Few respondents suggested that the causes lay in the economy. Although many said that jobs were less plentiful than normal during the recession, hardly any suggested that low-skilled jobs were simply unavailable. Nearly all rejected the idea that jobs had to be created through government before the men could work. Rather, the trouble was to find employers who would take a chance on men without a steady work history or who had just emerged from prison. There was clearly room in the economy for more low-skilled men to work, even if some lacked the organization to do it. That idea is plausible because the number of chronically nonworking men is small relative to the entire workforce, and there are large flows of workers into and out of jobs every month.

I asked respondents whether the men seemed more deterred from working by low wages or by the garnishing of their wages to pay child support. A strong majority said the latter. Fathers were discouraged to see their earnings cut by support deductions, but more important was their resentment at having to support spouses they had broken up with, through a system they perceived as unfair. Few officials suggested, therefore, that simply raising wages could be a solution to the work problem. More were attracted to the idea of guaranteeing jobs to the men in some form. The suggestion was not that jobs were otherwise unavailable but that a work program needed jobs it could be sure of, positions it could place men in immediately so that they would have to come to terms with working. Nevertheless, to create positions like this would take outside funding.

In child support, virtually all believed that nonpaying men had to be required to work in some form, not just offered the chance to do so. Respondents saw the men as a forgotten group deserving of more social attention, but at the same time programs had to have "teeth" if clients were to respond. "No calls, no shows," as one child support worker put it to me in Milwaukee. Criminal justice officials less often spoke of enforcing work through programs, yet work was still expected as a condition of parole. In both child support and criminal justice there also was support for paternalistic administration, where case managers supervised clients closely. A lot of men had missed such attention during their formative years, and they missed it again after they left work programs. One workforce official I talked to in San Antonio recalled an NCP Choices client who kept coming back to her and asking, "Can't you take me again?"

On the criminal justice side, respondents agreed that moving ex-offenders into jobs was essential to minimizing recidivism. To achieve this goal was the main motivation behind men's programs. Although the programs were aimed at parolees after release, officials also saw a need to begin reentry planning while men were still in prison. Respondents believed even more in barriers than did those in child support, one reason why attendance at work programs was usually left elective.

State Variations

The states I visited varied greatly in terms of degree of initiative, location, and dominant political tradition. Some of them were doing a lot in the men's work area, others little. They represented every region except the West. They included all three main political cultures found among the states—the "good government" tradition (Michigan and Wisconsin), big-city urban states (New Jersey, New York, and Ohio), and the South (Texas).[1] What had each recently done in men's work programming?

Michigan. A large manufacturing state in the upper Midwest, Michigan has been ravaged by job losses in the auto industry. Even in this severe setting, however, respondents generally affirmed that some jobs were available for low-skilled men who were supposed to work.

In child support, the state had not recently mounted work programs. In 2000–2001 it had used leftover TANF funds to serve some noncustodial parents, referring them either to the state's welfare work program or the workforce system. But follow-up was insufficient to assure attendance, and when funding lapsed, the program ended. Neither state CSE leaders nor local Friend of the Court agencies, which handle local child support enforcement, made a case to shift to state funding. However, in some counties Friend of the Court agencies still ran work programs for nonpaying men by using other monies, showing that support for this strategy was still strong. Some of these programs placed men in unpaid community service, while others paid special staff to refer them to local workforce agencies.

In prison reentry, in contrast, Michigan was a national leader. Following Governor Jennifer Granholm's election in 2002, the state launched the Michigan Prison Reentry Initiative (MPRI). MPRI aimed to reorient criminal justice away from a severe incarceration approach toward reentry. One motive was to save money on prisons, which were full and straining state budgets, but another was the conviction that community programs would in the end reduce crime as well as costs. The state had set up regional steering committees to plan local programs and sharply increased funding for these services. MPRI was not a work program per se, but it built up support for local work programs among other services. The initiative has so far cut the prison population and saved money, but it has also raised fears about public safety.[2]

New Jersey. A rich eastern state with a diverse economy, New Jersey has had no recent work initiatives in child support at the state level. Previously, there had been state work programs, one of them similar to Wisconsin's Children First, but they had faltered, chiefly due to a failure by the courts and the probation system to enforce men's attendance. An effective fatherhood program, however, was running in Mercer County, drawing on child support and other funding.

In prison reentry, the main state initiative was Another Chance, an experiment sponsored by Governor Jon Corzine to track 1,400 ex-offenders as they moved through the workforce system, where special job coaches were assigned to serve them. However, this program was separate from the regular prison or parole systems.

A more notable effort is the Newark Prisoner Reentry Initiative, in the state's largest city. This multiservice program for returning prisoners is supported mainly by federal grants. A related program, Operation Reconnect, is foundation funded and serves violent offenders who are excluded from federal funding. The Manhattan Institute, a conservative think tank in New York City, helped arrange funding and contributes some staff and oversight. The initiative has strong support from Newark mayor Cory Booker, who has made crime reduction a priority, but it has no integral connection to any of the mainstream criminal justice institutions.

New York. The third-largest state in population, New York is known for big government and liberal politics, centered on New York City. In child support, the state's main recent program is the Strengthening Families through Stronger Fathers Initiative, established by the Pataki administration. This effort funds pilot programs in five counties, including New York City, to provide services to low-income noncustodial parents. It also established a state refundable tax credit, part of the state's earned income tax credit, for low-income fathers provided they pay their judgments in full. These steps do not enforce work, although some counties, including New York City, have mandatory work programs to which judges may refer some nonpaying men.

In prison reentry, the state's Department of Criminal Justice Services (DCJS) has joined Transition from Prison to Community, a federal project to develop reentry services. With this funding, DCJS has established reentry task forces in twelve counties, not including New York City. This initiative does not involve state funding or reflect any reorientation of the state's larger criminal justice agencies, those for prisons, parole, and probation.

Ohio. Similar to Michigan, Ohio is a medium-sized midwestern state that has recently lost manufacturing jobs. In child support, CSE has not recently launched work programs from the state level. As in Michigan, it allowed counties to use unspent TANF funds to serve some of the employment needs of absent fathers, but this money had virtually disappeared since 2004.

More important is a prison diversion program funded by the Department of Rehabilitation and Corrections, the state's prison and parole agency. The department thought that too many men not paying child support, whom it viewed as minor offenders, were being convicted of criminal nonsupport and sent to prison, thus straining the state's prisons and budgets. So in 2007 it funded work programs run by child support agencies in seven counties to which hard-core nonpayers could be assigned in lieu of prison. This initiative had at least halted the rise in criminal nonpayers in prison. The department plans to expand the program to a further ten counties.

Meanwhile, the state is reforming the criminal justice system to give more emphasis to reentry, similar to the Michigan manner, but this shift has not yet led to an increase in services or a change in local organization comparable to MPRI. Work programs for ex-offenders were local.

Texas. The nation's second-largest state, Texas has a robust economy and has emerged as the leader in men's programming. It has work programs in both child support and criminal justice, and both have been favorably evaluated. Just as important, both are large scale and unusually well institutionalized, enjoying strong political support and stable administration and funding.

NCP Choices, the child support program, was described in chapter 3. It began in 2005 after years of struggle to improve child support compliance in the state. It is funded via TANF and run largely by the Texas Workforce Commission. It has a relatively simple structure. After men are remanded to the program by judges, special staff serve them at TWC, seeking mainly placement in private jobs. Project RIO, described in chapter 4, began in 1985. It has in-prison aspects, but outside of prison it resembles NCP Choices—it uses special workforce staff who seek jobs for ex-offenders, who are referred to the program by parole officers. It has lost some funding and been less prominent recently.

Wisconsin. An average-sized midwestern state, Wisconsin was a leader in welfare reform but has been less prominent in men's programming. Children First, discussed in chapter 3, was a work enforcement program for child support created in 1987 as part of welfare reform and implemented in much of the state in the 1990s. It has since suffered from limited funding.

In prison reentry, the Department of Corrections runs the Community Corrections Employment Program, which places ex-offenders in work-experience positions in public and nonprofit agencies. Because this program is small, the parole system relies chiefly on referring former prisoners to the workforce agencies. But that system is not oriented to work enforcement, and there is no special staff to help it serve the child support or ex-offender populations as in Texas.

Explaining State Differences

How do we explain the fact that some of these states are leaders in men's work programs and some are not? In chapter 5, we noted that the implementation of social programs varies *positively* with the amount of political will and money behind them and *negatively* with the degree of bureaucratic complexity. Consistent with that finding, a more detailed model drawn from welfare reform predicts that the implementation of men's work programs by states—in either child support or criminal justice—will vary with the following six factors. Three can be grouped under "political performance" and three under "administrative performance":

- **Political performance**

  Policymaking: Did elected officials take the lead in addressing the men's issue, or was the problem left to appointed officials?

  Consensus: Among political leaders, was there division or agreement about how to address the men's problem?

  Resources: Was the state willing and able to fund men's initiatives? Were funding arrangements stable or ad hoc?

- **Administrative performance**

  Commitment: Did senior administrators support men's initiatives, or did they simply comply with elected officials? Is the bureaucracy "on board" or resistant to change?

Coordination: Were the child support and/or criminal justice systems able to coordinate with each other and other agencies as necessary, such as welfare work programs, the workforce system, and outside contractors?

Capability: Did the bureaucracy have the capacities needed to run men's work programs, particularly in case management and reporting systems?[3]

Differences in these six factors explain quite well which of the six states have led in men's programming and which have not.

Policymaking. The extent of change was most clearly related to the attention given to men's issues by elected leaders. In Michigan, the dramatic MPRI stemmed directly from Governor Granholm's election in 2002. The previous governor, Republican John Engler, had supported severe incarceration as the best answer to crime. But this policy had filled the prisons, creating strong budgetary pressure to change course. The attraction of reentry was that it might permit minimizing incarceration in favor of community services. Granholm had run on this issue, among others, so her election generated a mandate for change. Her brain trust on this issue included Patricia Caruso, Dennis Schrantz, and Jeff Padden.

Upon Granholm's inauguration, Caruso and Schrantz became director and deputy director, respectively, of the state Department of Corrections. Padden, a consultant and former state legislator, remained an important adviser. This team proceeded to retrain and reorient the department toward a reentry approach. Their first steps were to build up funding for reentry services at the local level, as this would generate the saving in prison space that was most urgent. MPRI also involved improved prerelease preparation in the prisons and more effective risk assessment of prisoners for parole, but these elements were less urgent. Granholm was reelected in 2006. The current Department of Corrections leadership hopes to have implemented these changes by the time the governor leaves office in 2011.

In Texas, the success of NCP Choices also reflected top-level political attention. CSE had originally been delegated to the state welfare department, which in turn contracted it out to the state's 254 counties, producing complexity and low performance. In 1983–85, child support was centralized in the Office of the Attorney General (OAG), giving it more visibility, and then was reorganized again within OAG in 1994.[4] Following the initial implementation of NCP Choices, OAG persuaded the legislature to expand, on the argument that the investment would be recouped in more child support collections.

In Ohio, the diversion program funded by the Department of Rehabilitation and Corrections reflected an emphasis on agency collaboration pressed by Governor Ted Strickland, who was elected in 2006. Carri Brown served on Strickland's transition team and then was appointed deputy director of child support in the state welfare department. She pursued a broader collaboration involving child support, the prison agency, and welfare.

In Wisconsin, men's issues obtained top-level political attention as long as Children First was part of Governor Tommy Thompson's ambitious welfare reform. After Thompson left office, attention waned, and the state never fully implemented work programs in child support.

In New Jersey and New York, political leaders have not seriously focused on the men's issue. New Jersey's Another Chance was a gubernatorial initiative, as was New York's Strengthening Families through Stronger Fathers, but both involved too little change in the regular child support and criminal justice agencies to amount to much. Agency leaders lacked the political backing to challenge established routines and institutionalize new programs as they had done in Ohio, Michigan, and Texas.

Consensus. In general, men's programming was less divisive than welfare reform had been. In Congress, the welfare work demands of PRWORA outraged many, yet the same legislation contained far-reaching changes to toughen child support enforcement, and these passed with little dissent. At the state level, too, child support was less visible than benefit programs. Those running the child support system often recognized the need to change, making innovation easier.

Criminal justice reform was somewhat more contentious. In Michigan, Republicans were most aligned with the old lock-'em-up policies, whereas Democrats favored the shift toward reentry. The issue engaged the public somewhat more than child support problems. The prospect that more offenders might be served in the community, rather than behind bars, raised fears of recidivism. Some conservatives played on those fears to resist change. Yet at the same time, the fiscal pressures that drove change in Michigan and Ohio were bipartisan. In Ohio, the legislature was closely divided on the issue, and the split cut across party lines.

Criminal justice issues also provoked more division because administrators were less open to change. In child support, work programs meant improved enforcement and to this degree aligned with agency ethos. In criminal justice, expanded work programs smacked of relaxed enforcement, helping out the undeserving, thus challenging hard-line traditions. Prison and parole chieftains took credit for the recent decline in crime, asserting that incarceration had helped to achieve it. They were less aware of the limitations of that strategy than were outside experts and the communities heavily impacted by incarceration and reentry. Their flank could be turned only by top-level political change, as happened in Michigan.

Resources. As explained further in chapter 9, federal funding for men's programs has been limited. Thus, implementation was strongly dependent on state resources. The states with the most ambitious programs also provided the most secure funding. Some arrangements were ad hoc. Texas had to arrange backdoor funding of NCP Choices from TANF, although this limited the program to serving noncustodial parents with a welfare connection. The Ohio diversion program depended on unusual funding from the prison agency. In criminal justice, funding is committed to established prisons, parole, and probation systems. Rarely is there a major initiative such as MPRI that makes substantial new money available. Uncertain funding largely explained the rapid turnover of programs that surfaced in the state survey.

Officials in several states said that one obstacle to larger mandatory work programs was a lack of jail or prison space to enforce the requirements. Faced with limits, judges and prosecutors preferred to lock up violent criminals rather than child support defaulters, who, as mentioned earlier, they often viewed as minor offenders. States also needed jail space or halfway houses for reentry programs, as a means of penalizing noncompliance short of sending men back to prison. These facilities also involved resources.

The prospect of improved collections helped NCP Choices officials sell expansion to the Texas legislature. This sort of case, unfortunately, is harder to make for reentry programs. Here the gains are not as visible or immediate.

They come indirectly from permitting reduced incarceration and, in the long term, reducing crime. Making that connection depends on evaluations and cost-benefit analyses. For budget officials or legislators saying "show me," that is a harder sell.

Commitment. Largely, men's programs have to be crafted out of existing institutions—child support officials, judges, parole officers, and workforce agencies working together. Getting the leaders of all these groups on board was crucial to getting programs to function on the ground.

NCP Choices was built on a close collaboration between the Office of the Attorney General, in charge of CSE, and the Texas Workforce Commission. Senior officials in both agencies designed NCP Choices together and then sold it to child support judges, who agreed to supervise men's referrals to the program. This "three-legged stool," as one of them described it, had weathered the strains of working together, chiefly through creative management and problem solving by OAG.

As mentioned earlier, the workforce system in most states has not been attuned to enforcing work. That seriously impeded the implementation of welfare reform in Texas and other states. But TWC had come around to accept the need for enforcement in both TANF and child support. Far from fearing to serve disadvantaged men, TWC saw them as good prospects to generate placements and satisfy WIA's job-entry targets, exactly because they *had* to participate.

In Ohio, alongside the diversion program funded by the Department of Rehabilitation and Corrections, child support officials convened a task force to improve collaboration among that agency, welfare, and criminal justice. Local CSE directors also participated. The group recommended that each agency learn more about the others. The agencies could also work together on legislative issues, such as reducing the buildup of child support arrears when noncustodial fathers went to prison.[5] But this effort, though helpful, fell well short of the deeper meshing of goals and operations seen in Texas. As a result, the diversion program, while successful, aimed largely to ease child support's pressure on the prisons and did not address the men's problem more generally. In Michigan, MPRI achieved collaboration largely at the local level, where the regional steering committees were to contact various public and private agencies.

In the other states, what stood out is the disengagement of much of the bureaucracy from the men's problem. The workforce and parole systems went about their business without focusing on the need to raise work levels among men in general. In Wisconsin, for instance, workforce officials defined the low-income men's problem as a lack of specific job skills, downplaying any need to enforce work. That stance left work program proponents isolated. CSE or a CEO could still create effective work programs, but they will be small and peripheral to the main institutions.

For child support work programs, judges are a lion in the path. Much of their discretion in deciding paternity and child support orders has been circumscribed by OCSE administrators and federal rules. Today, their more important role is in overseeing men's compliance. Child support officials often value this involvement, as judges' orders have special authority with the men. Drug courts and other specialized courts take this role to an extreme, immersing the judge in the details of individual men's lives. Some judges identify with that role. One judge I met in Ohio described himself as a "father" to his men, whom he called his "children."

But other judges resist this role. Enforcement is not what they put on the black robe to do. In New York City, some judges have refused to refer men to the local child support work program, viewing it as ineffective. There have been recent improvements as the two sides worked out differences. In New Jersey, judges accepted enforcement in principle but resisted playing that role themselves, forcing the cancelation of state programs. In Texas, judges also resisted child support work programs prior to NCP Choices. They came around only after OAG convinced them there was no other way to get compliance. Even so, OAG has had to get the judges on board in each region of the state as the program has expanded.

Coordination. Even if agencies endorse a work program in principle, are they able to coordinate their operations? Many small changes in agency routines are required. Probably the most important are in reporting systems. Staff in different agencies have to be able to access the same information about a case at their computers, yet their information systems often conflict. In Texas, one key to NCP Choices was the development of a "bridge" between the OAG and TWC computers—the Choices Online Tracking System, or COLTS. This system allowed quick referral of men from the courts to TWC, with quick notice back to OAG and judges should men fail to appear. In the Ohio collaboration, one recommendation was that child support and criminal justice work on "data matching" to permit the same sort of joint system.

Referral of clients between agencies is a threat to participation, as clients can easily "fall between the cracks" and never make it from one office to another. Many respondents told me that when judges ordered men into work programs it was crucial that a workforce staff person be literally in the courtroom to "take the handoff." If the men had to find the workforce office on their own, they would often fail to. In the Ohio diversion programs, some personnel in the Department of Rehabilitation and Corrections were outstationed at workforce centers to connect with clients there. In paternalistic programs, clients are motivated by relationships with staff, who in turn must relate securely to each other. Only then, like parents in a family, can staff give a consistent message about expectations.

This need to collaborate raises the danger of bureaucratic conflicts. One key to Project RIO was working out the division of labor between parole officers and the workforce staffs to whom they referred parolees. Officials drafted detailed memoranda setting out each agency's expectations of the other. Managers journeyed to local offices to sort out conflicts. Parole officers came to view the workforce staff not as rivals but as allies to whom they could safely delegate the employment function.[6]

In less institutionalized settings, none of these linkages have been built, and a program is isolated. The Newark Prison Reentry Initiative, for example, has political support and funding, but it lacks smooth-running ties to the local child support and parole systems. Operation Reconnect is seeking to reach out to these agencies and craft a common data system. Building these ties is much of what implementation requires.

Capability. One key capability agencies need for work programs is the joint reporting systems described above. The other is improved case management. CSE already employs staff with caseloads of nonpaying cases that they are supposed to "work" to get all the collections they can. Criminal justice already has parole officers who enforce the rules of parole. But as we have seen, neither of these systems usually focuses on work as a central goal.

Work programs create, in effect, a second set of case managers who focus much more on employment. That role is played by the workforce system in the Texas programs and by special case managers, funded by the Department of Rehabilitation and Corrections, in the Ohio diversion programs. It is also played by the work crew supervisors in CEO, who in effect replace the parole officers as the chief overseers of their clients. Case management is also developing at the local level as part of the MPRI in Michigan.

Compared to the former overseers, the new case managers are more proactive and client centered. They spend less time sitting at their desks and requiring that clients comply with the rules of their systems, although they still enforce rules. They spend more time out in the field actively helping men get and keep jobs, taking them to job interviews, and sorting out other problems. Will this new style evaluate well? CEO's results, at least, are encouraging.

Another important tactic is voluntary outreach. In Milwaukee and Detroit, I encountered creative child support managers who had largely given up on individualized enforcement of child support. Faced with huge caseloads and limited staff, they could not hope to improve collections by dragging men individually into court. Rather, they held breakfasts, lunches, and open houses to attract men owing child support, teach them about the system, and exhort them to comply with it voluntarily. Do that, they promised, and in return we will help you with visitation rights and arrears. And they have had some success.

Conclusion

What stands out about the more ambitious states is *alignment*. The political and bureaucratic pieces have come together to create new institutions. There is firm political support for enforcing and promoting work, and administrators have developed the procedures and collaboration needed to do that. A clearer message has also formed about what these states expect from poor men, although we are still far from the implementation needed to trigger spontaneous compliance and diversion.

History helps to explain why particular states achieve this success. Wisconsin became the leading state in welfare reform in part because it had been a leader in national social policy development for a century. Within the state as well, the leading counties were those who had pursued welfare reform for some time, often failing before they succeeded.[7] In the men's area, too, heritage matters. Michigan was also a prominent welfare reformer, and in prison reform it has been even bolder. MPRI was not created overnight. It was nurtured by its proponents over decades and then implemented through years of bureaucratic toil.

In Texas, the architects of NCP Choices failed for years to develop effective work programs before they succeeded. Those hard lessons helped to forge the agreements among the agencies and judges that undergird the program today. Texas has a reputation for severity in both child support and criminal justice. However, that history has also made the state wrestle longer than most with how to integrate low-performing men. A conservative culture also causes Texans to take that mission seriously. They are particularly uncomfortable with men who fail at the traditional male role of working, and they take steps to change that. The state has labored long and hard for the successes it has today.

As I noted in the introduction, social policy ultimately is embedded in institutions. The true solution to poverty is statecraft—the meshing of politics and administration to create new structures that can promote and enforce key values such as work. Effective reformers are those who realize policy "on the ground," who build up consensus and routines, to the point where society changes.

8

Recommendations

The discussion thus far establishes that work is central to poor men's problems. To raise work levels will take work enforcement as well as new benefits. Existing evaluations suggest that work programs can help to solve the work problem, provided they are well implemented. The state survey and fieldwork also show that programs are in fact being implemented and something about how.

Based on all of the above, this chapter sets out a preferred model for these programs. I recommend a mandatory program aimed mainly at achieving and sustaining work in available jobs. I also estimate costs. Some program design issues are unresolved at this point. I also discuss wage subsidies that, ideally, should be combined with the new programs to form a new regime for low-income men.

Desirable Features

Low-income men owing child support or parolees obligated to work would initially be subject to the regular child support and parole systems, as now. But if they persistently failed to work steadily, they would be assigned to a mandatory work program where they would face much closer supervision. Whenever they established steady work, they would return to the looser oversight of the regular institutions. These work programs should preferably have the following features.

Mandatoriness. Past work programs for men have been both mandatory and voluntary. In practice, some programs have drawn both volunteers and others on mandatory referral from child support or parole authorities. The enrollment problems of most of these programs seem to me decisive against a voluntary approach. No benefits, however generous, seem sufficient to entice seriously nonworking men to come forward and address their problems. Even the New Hope Project in Milwaukee, which offered a rich package of benefits to low-income adults in return for working thirty hours a week, had great difficulty filling its rolls, even among jobless men.[1] In Texas, officials say firmly that the main reason NCP Choices has outperformed earlier child support enforcement programs is that participation is better enforced.

We also know from welfare reform that clients who volunteer for a work program are the least likely—due to selection effects—to gain much from it. Many of them are likely to go to work on their own, even without a program. The more reluctant eligibles can profit more from a program, but they will not come forward unless required. Enforcement was also critical for generating welfare reform's large diversion effects. For men's work programs to have any comparable ambition, they too must enforce participation. The programs should be open to volunteers, but administrators should expect to fill their ranks mainly through mandatory referrals from child support judges or parole officers.

Case Management. Work programs should include case managers who supervise clients personally. The men need overseers not only to help them access benefits and opportunities but also to be sure they maintain participation and fulfill their assignments. Much of that need reflects their isolation and powerlessness.[2] In contrast to existing oversight under either child support or criminal justice, supervision must be targeted much more specifically on working, and it must be more immediate. The supervisor must leave his or her desk and monitor actual work or job search and must have some immediate way to reward good behavior and penalize bad. The goal is to be sure that men look for work consistently and keep jobs once found. The precedent is drug programs, where swift and certain, not severe, punishment is what motivates compliance.[3]

Case management can take many forms, from CEO's work crew supervisors to Ready4Work's mentors. One promising approach is halfway houses or day reporting centers where ex-offenders are closely supervised as they undergo drug treatment and then seek jobs. Men earn greater rewards and freedoms within the institution only as they meet program expectations, especially by becoming reliably employed. This approach appears to reduce recidivism and raise work levels sharply, although serious evaluations have yet to be done.[4]

Work First. Work programs should aim above all to place clients in available jobs and keep them there. Work first does not mean work only. Programs may well include an orientation to work, as at CEO. They could also include some short-term training to qualify clients for desirable positions that are clearly available. But the dominant focus must be on coming to terms with the labor market as it is, not training for better jobs sometime in the future.

Programs must clearly communicate that their purposes are to get men to work and pay child support. A problem with PFS was that its goals were too complicated, even in conflict. It aimed to improve not only men's child support payments but also their earnings and ties to families. The emphasis was more on being served and trained than actually working and paying.[5] In the end, the program did not clearly enforce anything except participation. It seemed to reward declining to work and declining to pay more than doing so.

A better idea is to enforce work and child support payment and condition any benefits on compliance with these norms. That is what New Hope did, by making work the ticket to benefits. This is what CEO does with its upfront work demands, followed by job placement and attention to other problems. And the benefits received are no better than similar workers receive outside the program. The program promises not to shield participants from ordinary obligations but to fulfill them and thereby open up wider opportunities. NCP Choices appears to outperform PFS largely because it aims simply at work. It does not remit men's child support obligations. The message is clear that the program is about fulfilling responsibilities, not setting them aside.

The argument to include more remediation is simply that poor men are typically so unskilled. Without some effort to improve skills, some ask, how can these men hope to get jobs good enough to support families? But in PFS, offering very disadvantaged men training proved difficult because the training agencies or employers viewed them as unqualified. The men themselves often resisted training because of a felt need for immediate income.[6] PFS erred in defining the men's problem as a lack of human capital. Rather, the problem is a lack of basic work discipline. The goal for these men should be to establish a steady work history, after which many employers will be willing to train them. The way forward is through low-wage jobs rather than around them.

Also, the idea of training as something separate from work now seems outdated. Training tends to connote skills learned in stand-alone education or training programs apart from jobs. But research has shown that most people learn new skills mainly on the job, not separately. So for most people, the best way to improve skills and move up is to work steadily in available positions.[7] In addition, many poor adults would rather do that than go back to school, where many have failed.

Up through the early 1990s, most experts believed that the best way to get poor mothers working and off welfare was first to assign them to education or training to raise their skills so they could get better jobs. But few of them proved able to finish training programs, and fewer still went to work afterward. Work policy began to bite only in the later 1990s, when work was demanded in available jobs. That raised employment and earnings by much more than training did because it got women working more consistently. The most successful programs, as in Portland, Oregon, retained an element of training, but it was short term and did not compromise a strong work focus.[8]

For men, the equivalent must be to get clients working (and paying child support) as quickly as possible, with only short delays, if any, to enhance skills. Their wages may be inadequate to supporting families, but the answer is not to decline low-paying jobs in hope of better ones. Rather, it is to subsidize available jobs as needed, but conditional on working and paying one's child support.

Assured Employment. Any idea of enforcing work assumes that work is available to those facing the requirement. In welfare reform, jobs proved plentiful, and jobs were created on a large scale only in special situations.[9] In the case of men, there is more concern that jobs may be lacking. Men with a felony record are barred from holding many jobs. Unskilled men are more threatening than women, and some employers refuse to hire ex-offenders.[10]

Therefore, to enforce work, jobs will ultimately have to be guaranteed to men who fail to find their own. Such assurance would remove excuses and increase community pressure on nonworking men to accept employment.[11] Assignment to guaranteed jobs would also "smoke out" men who appear jobless but are really working illegally.

Politically, it is important that guaranteed jobs be seen as obligations for the client, not as a gift or benefit. These jobs are not in the mold of the positions given away in the 1970s under the Comprehensive Employment and Training Act. Those were often higher paid, more comfortable jobs, many of them taken by municipal employees who had been furloughed. Jobs for child support defaulters or ex-offenders cannot be seen as better than jobs for workers who appear more deserving. The positions would also need to be productive, not punitive or make-work. At the same time, they would have to be time limited, pay only the minimum wage, be largely confined to manual work, and entail stiff oversight. CEO is one model.

Postplacement Follow-Up. Low-skilled men often have more trouble keeping jobs than finding them. Due to the defensiveness discussed in chapter 2, many of these men are offended too easily by bosses or coworkers and end up being fired or just leaving. Thus, effective work programs should include "extended case management"—staff who visit clients on the job after placement and help to work out problems that may threaten job retention.

NCP Choices follows up with clients for six months after placement. This is another difference from PFS that may explain the newer program's improved employment results. CEO has built a similar capacity to improve retention in private jobs following its transitional positions.

Help with Other Problems. Although employment must be the center of any men's work program, the clients do have other problems that often impede working, for example, ill health or lack of housing. In welfare reform, the presumption originally was that "barriers" to employment, such as lack of skills or health problems, had to be overcome before mothers could be expected to work. The 1990s proved that many mothers who had seemed unemployable could and would work once the expectation was clear.

That experience suggests that problems should preferably be addressed in the context of working rather than in advance of it. The style of both CEO and America Works is to put men to work quickly and then to deal with other difficulties as they emerge. This way, claims to incapacity do not automatically become an excuse not to work. Special attention is not given to men as a right, up front, but rather in return for functioning. That approach is more consistent with the psychology of men, who deeply desire to *earn* what they get.

Of the programs we have surveyed, CEO and America Works probably come closest to this model. Both involve mandatory referral of ex-offenders from the prisons or parole, case management, a work-first emphasis, some form of assured employment, postplacement follow-up, and attention to other needs. Both, of course, are as yet only local programs.

Of the larger programs reviewed, PFS lacked a work-first emphasis, and the fatherhood programs were largely voluntary. Both NCP Choices and Project RIO focus narrowly on employment, but neither guarantees jobs nor addresses other problems explicitly. Instead, placement staff deal informally with personal difficulties and refer clients to other agencies as needed.[12] State child support officials recognize a need for "wraparound services," such as drug or mental health treatment, to support the work mission.

Some other experts have proposed a program model similar to mine. Jeremy Travis would put more ex-offenders to work in prison and then after release put them in community work programs modeled on Project RIO or CEO. Work would be enforced by closer supervision while other problems, such as drug addiction, were addressed. Bruce Western, one of the designers of ComALERT, has recently proposed a reentry program combining features of that program with CEO.[13] Another close analogue is the Doe Fund's Ready, Willing, and Able, which combines work with other services, although this program is voluntary.

The more service-oriented programs considered above, such as the fatherhood programs, appear less promising as a model for the future. That is partly because their impacts are unclear but mostly because they are voluntary when it is manifest that programs must be mandatory to succeed. However, an element of outreach to poor men may be essential to achieve participation, even if programs are mandatory. The suasions behind work enforcement should be kept personal and informal to the extent possible. In this, the fatherhood programs have had useful experience.

Costs

At a time of fiscal stringency, could government afford work programs for men? How much they would cost will vary with the model and other details. The estimates I give below are only rough. But in all cases it is reasonably clear that the programs would save money for government overall *if* well implemented.

The nearest precedent for large-scale mandatory work programs for poor adults is probably welfare reform, where in a few cases government created jobs on a large scale. On the one hand, welfare work programs have to pay for child care, but on the other hand the mothers need not be paid beyond the welfare they already receive. In workfare programs in the early 1990s, costs per filled position ranged from $681 to $8,168 annually, with each slot supporting several recipients over a year.[14] In New York City's Work Experience Program in the late 1990s, the cost was $9,429 per slot.[15]

A Men's Program. Compared to welfare mothers, men must be paid wages to work but seldom require child care, so costs appear to be roughly similar. In the National Supported Work Demonstration, which guaranteed jobs to disadvantaged job seekers, costs for ex-offenders were $4,637 per client in the late 1970s.[16] Currently, America Works is paid up to $4,250 to place each client in jobs, with the amount varying with how long the jobs last. Wages are off budget, paid by private employers. CEO's costs are much higher—$35,029 per slot annually—because it has to pay for wages as well as supervision and overhead. But because the program also sells its services to the agencies where it works, net cost per slot is only $3,850, or $642 per client, because an average of six clients occupy each slot annually.[17]

Chapter 1 estimated the number of men who need work enforcement at 1.2 million. Using America Works's costs, the tab for a national program would be $3.4 billion a year, assuming each man is served once.[18] For CEO it would be $775 million if each slot serves six clients, $4.6 billion if each served one. CEO's transitional jobs are probably too short to maximize impact (see below), so the number of clients served per slot would probably have to be fewer than six. Thus, the CEO's costs on a national basis would probably fall somewhere between the per-slot and per-client figures.

Bruce Western's cost estimates are not strictly comparable because he assumes fewer clients (partly because he covers only ex-offenders). He assumes employment would cost around $15,000 per client or $5.5 billion a year, higher than other estimates because placements would be in paid positions and last up to a year. He adds other elements—housing, drug treatment, in-prison programming, and expanded access to TANF and Pell grants—for a total cost of $8.4 billion.[19]

Offsets. Such costs are not prohibitive, and they are offset by certain gains for government and society. With workfare programs in welfare, the budget cost in most cases was partially repaid in savings in welfare and other benefits and then more than recouped if a value was placed on the services produced. In New York's Work Experience Program, net value was estimated at $756 to $15,896 per slot, depending on how various items were valued.[20]

For men, work enforcement should lead to gains in child support collections. As Table 1-1 shows, some $12 billion in child support went uncollected in 2005. Existing evaluations did not assess rigorously how fully child support gains offset costs, but the potential for gains means that child support work programs probably can be cost-effective.[21] That belief helped motivate the expansion of NCP Choices in Texas.

The verdict is clearer in criminal justice. The National Supported Work Demonstration placed several groups of disadvantaged men in transitional jobs. Whether the program paid for itself in the case of ex-offenders depends on how one estimates the resulting changes in criminal activity.[22] But these clients were already out of prison and not on parole. For men still under supervision, savings would be greater because work programs—again, if effective—would reduce technical violations and returns to prison. Western estimates these savings alone at more than $4 billion a year. With other offsets, his program would generate $10.8 billion in benefits, more than outweighing its costs.[23] As mentioned in chapter 4, CEO generated substantially greater benefits than costs.

The larger point is that incarceration is enormously expensive. The average state spent an estimated $27,536 per inmate in 2008.[24] That figure is much larger than virtually all of the per-client cost figures given above. Thus, if a work policy could justify even small reductions in imprisonment, the savings would easily pay for the programs, perhaps several times over.[25] The Project RIO evaluation found that the program diverted nearly 20 percent of its clients from prison in 1990. To incarcerate them would have cost $20 million, but the program cost only $4 million, a savings of more than $15 million. If we take its outcomes for impacts, Ready4Work also saved money, as it cost $4,500 per participant as against many times this for incarceration.[26] The potential to save money helps explain the growth of Project RIO in Texas and prison reentry reforms in Michigan and Ohio.

Those savings would come not only from reduced revocations of parole but also from shorter sentences served behind bars. More convicts could serve more of their sentences on parole—if it were clear that assignment to work programs would reduce recidivism. Although work release requires spending more on parole supervision, this cost is more than offset by reduced incarceration.[27] With more parolees, the number of crimes parolees committed would no doubt rise. That is visible and controversial. The hope is that society would accept it because overall crime rates would fall. That faith is crucial to the whole reentry project.[28]

Unresolved Issues

Some issues of program design and implementation are unresolved due to the limited experience we have with men's work programs to date. Below are some concerns that need to be addressed.

Guaranteed Jobs. It seems necessary to ensure jobs if one is to enforce work on men. But, as mentioned earlier, my field respondents did not generally think a work guarantee was necessary or feasible. They might think this way because guarantees cost money that is not now available and because work programs are still small. If the programs grew, as recommended, private jobs might become insufficient to place all the men involved. The number of employers willing to hire these men, especially ex-offenders, may simply be too small.[29]

Even if one thinks jobs must be guaranteed, the best way to do this is also unclear. The program can create positions itself, as CEO and Wisconsin's

Community Corrections Employment Program do, although CEO also sells its services in a manner akin to private contractors. But it may be cheaper to rely on repeated placement in the private sector, as America Works does, although then the work guarantee is less explicit. The evaluations of both programs, when complete, should shed light on this issue.

How long transitional jobs must last is also unclear. CEO's are short, usually limited to seventy-five days. The program might have better retention in private placements if the slots lasted longer. In welfare reform, unpaid work assignments for welfare mothers have typically lasted about twelve to thirteen weeks. In the National Supported Work Demonstration, ex-offenders typically spent 5.2 months in arranged jobs, which could last up to a year.[30] CEO counters that whether men can adjust to working is usually clear well before seventy-five days and that longer positions would cost more.

Sanctions. To make work mandatory, men must suffer some penalty if they fail to participate. But what should that be? In welfare work programs, it was loss of welfare benefits. That sanction proved insufficient to prevent many mothers leaving welfare without working. The sanction in men's programs would appear to be much tougher because men who refuse a work assignment can be thrown in jail for contempt (for child support nonpayers) or sent back to prison (for parolees). But invoking this sanction has higher costs than in the welfare case. One must pay to incarcerate the offenders, and doing so interrupts whatever training or rehabilitation programs they may have begun.

The parole system has worked hard to develop penalties that can enforce compliance without sending men back to prison. The options include fining the noncompliant, making them report to parole officers more often (such as day reporting systems), or confining them in community facilities for a few days, short of a full return to prison. So far, such systems have not shown that they truly stave off incarceration. More development is needed.[31]

The meaning of sanctioning was far clearer in welfare reform—a denial of benefits—but invoking penalties was also sensitive because it seemed to put children at risk. With men, the sanction for nonwork is less defined but also less controversial. At the local level, few dispute that men who violate their obligations should face consequences. The issue is not whether to enforce work but how to do it with the least cost, both human and financial.

Size of Program. Most men's work programs are now quite small. To have more impact, they have to grow, but how much? Would it be practicable to assign to work programs *all* men who incur contempt of court for nonpayment of child support, rather than only the most difficult cases? Mandatory work would then become a recognized penalty for repeated noncompliance. In criminal justice, perhaps *all* felons being released from prison should go into a work program for a short period, as at CEO. The fact that CEO's impacts were greatest for men who came to the program within three months of leaving prison argues for this approach. These steps would be costly, but there would also be offsetting gains in child support collections and reductions in incarceration, to judge from the evaluations. Where to position the tradeoff must hinge on further experience, evaluations, and cost-benefit analyses.

Role of Contractors. It is clear that men's programs have to draw more authority and support from the mainstream child support and criminal justice systems if they are to have impact. But must they be operated directly by those agencies? In welfare reform, the trend has been to vest the work mission in private contractors. That permits flexibility and accountability, but it also makes it less clear who is in charge. Programs become more complicated and thus more difficult for clients to navigate. Communication problems across multiple units increase.

The trial programs assessed in chapters 3 and 4 were already heavily based on contracting. Most men's programs make some use of the workforce system, which itself uses private vendors. During interviews, some child support and criminal justice officials said that they preferred to contract out the work mission because their own personnel were unsuited to it. Thus, contracting might speed up implementation. However, it might also shield the parent agencies from truly internalizing the work mission, as they need to do.

A Joint Program? Because the populations of child support defaulters and ex-offenders overlap, having the child support and criminal justice systems run a joint work program might yield economies of scale. In Ohio, the two systems were already collaborating to run prison diversion programs, and in Texas both used the workforce system to serve their clients in a similar way. On the other hand, in most localities, the child support system seems readier to accept a work mission than does the criminal justice system. The ex-offender population on average is also more disadvantaged than child support nonpayers and hence more in need of ancillary services such as health and housing. Those differences might make a joint program impractical.

Sustainability. A challenge for all antipoverty programs is maintaining their vitality over time. Caring for the poor is demanding. Staffs that interact with them tend to suffer burnout. To protect themselves, they often cease truly to engage with people and just go through the motions impersonally.[32] After their initial successes, Children First in Wisconsin, Project RIO in Texas, and the Ceasefire anticrime initiative in Boston seem to have suffered from declining energy.

However, putting men to work is probably less demanding than more intimate interventions, such as family preservation programs. By its nature, employment creates another authority—the employer—to share the oversight role. There is also strong public support for the work mission, so political leaders are likely to give the effort more support and attention than some other programming. That encourages staffs to persevere. Work programs are also relatively easy to monitor because their output—job placements—is relatively easy to define and measure. To succeed over time, men's programs, like welfare, will still need committed managers and administrators.

These uncertainties all reflect our inexperience with men's programs, including limited research. One aim of national policy, addressed below, must be to expand what we know.

The Benefit Side

Helping poor men, like welfare mothers, seems to require a combination of help and hassle. Some effort is needed to raise unskilled men's wages, both for their benefit and to establish with the political class that work enforcement is not punitive.

This effort would change the one-sided way society now deals with these men. Currently, the government usually gives benefits to mothers and children but not to absent fathers. In principle at least, welfare reform made cash aid conditional on the mother working, though other benefits such as Medicaid and Food Stamps remain entitlements. The father can get only Food Stamps, if needy, yet has to work and pay support to families he may never see. PFS recognized this asymmetry but failed, in the end, to overcome it. Neither the obligations nor the benefits it defined were clear enough.[33]

Wage subsidies hitched to working and paying support would make both obligations and benefits a lot clearer. Now society would be giving poor men cold cash—but in return for highly specific expectations. The prospect of immediate payment for labor is one of the secrets of CEO's large, if transient, employment impacts. Some might prefer to pay the men weekly or monthly rather than daily lest the money be wasted. But above all, this benefit comes *through working*; it is not, as in PFS, something separate.

Wage subsidies could accompany work enforcement programs but could not substitute for them. In 2006, as part of the Strengthening Families through Stronger Fathers Initiative, New York recently instituted an improved wage subsidy for noncustodial parents who pay their judgments, but few eligibles have claimed the benefit, and the gains in payments are very small.[34] That experience confirms earlier evidence, reviewed above, that work incentives do little to raise work levels. A failure to respond strongly to incentives is typical of this population.

The idea of combining the father's work with a public subsidy has some affinities to Irwin Garfinkel's idea of a Child Support Assurance System (CSAS).[35] As in CSAS, a subsidy would in practice pay much of the cost of child support. But in CSAS, the work and subsidy bore on different people— the father still had to work and pay support while the mother received the subsidy and could work or not as she chose. It was a version of entitlement that proved politically unacceptable. Here, instead, subsidy and work bear on the same person. The father gets a subsidy only if he works and also pays his judgment. In CSAS, government replaced the father, supporting the family if he failed. Here, government empowers the father, both requiring him to pay and rewarding him when he does.

Gordon Berlin and Wendell Primus, among others, have recently advanced proposals for wage subsidies along these lines. In 2010, the earned income tax credit subsidy rate for a worker without dependents was only 7.65 percent, and the maximum amount was only $457.[36] The Berlin proposal would raise that to 25 percent and nearly $2,000, respectively, but it would cost $29 billion to $33 billion a year. The cost is much more than for work programs because 35 million low-income workers could be eligible, not just the much smaller numbers subject to work requirements. To reduce the subsidy to 20 percent would halve the cost.[37]

The nearest precedent for the proposed scheme is New Hope, which conditioned a rich set of benefits for low-income men (among other poor and near-poor adults) on working thirty hours a week. The project had difficulty recruiting clients, and it raised their work effort only slightly. In the proposed system, however, the men would be obligated to work and pay support on pain, ultimately, of incarceration, so their participation and work effort should be higher. New Hope's case managers did an excellent job of not only helping clients to work but also persuading them to put in the thirty hours to get the benefits. Here the staffs should ideally be just as helpful, but they would have more authority.[38] The result would be what David Riemer has called an Employment Maintenance Organization—a body charged with keeping poor adults employed.[39]

A further benefit that might follow from working and paying is adjustments in the men's child support arrears. If a father paid his current judgment steadily, states might choose to abate some of his debt to government for supporting his family. Some proposals in Congress would require that states consider this. To remit debt recognizes the interest society has in fathers working regularly, beyond just supporting families. Arrearages become a resource, another basis for work enforcement. The mother might also remit some of the arrearages she is owed, but this would be voluntary.

Men for Themselves

Hitherto, interest in poor men has been motivated chiefly by a desire to get more money for families. The men were seen chiefly as fathers who ought to be supporting their children, if necessary through child support. But if we believe the view of male psychology set out earlier, men need to succeed at work for their own benefit. Indeed, they usually cannot succeed as family men unless they first succeed on the job, to their own and others' satisfaction. Were they to do that, the whole need for child support would recede.

Welfare reform had the effect of driving most welfare mothers away from government into the private sector, where most have supported themselves without cash aid, although many still rely on Food Stamps or Medicaid. The proposed men's regime, however, would draw clients *toward* government. They would have to accept working and paying into the official tax and child support systems while also drawing benefits in return. In these senses, government would grow, although poverty and social problems should decline.

Focusing on men for themselves does not mean taking their side in the battles over child support and other family issues. Whether child support obligations should be cut or conditioned on visitation rights, for example, are separate issues.[40] The point is only that men need help to fulfill their obligations, whatever those are. These men need first to succeed in the workplace. If they do that, their responsibilities to families will tend to take care of themselves. To build up their capacities on the job is in everyone's interests.

9

National Policy

For reducing poverty, men's work programs are worth backing, but it is too soon to mandate them on the states as Congress did with work obligations in welfare. The evaluation evidence supporting them is not as strong as it was for welfare work programs. Political leaders have also paid less attention to low-income men than they did to welfare, and the institutions that now serve men are less ready for change, although they are moving that way.

Rather, national policy should seek cautious expansion of men's programs while learning more about them. The federal government should support states that are ready to move forward, such as Michigan and Texas, but not yet require that all states do so. The main needs are for steadier funding and more evaluation. On the benefit side, the tax credits for low-income men should be expanded but conditioned on work and child support payment. Congress has taken steps in these directions, but I suggest some changes. The greatest need is simply for vision—for the daring to create a general work expectation for poor men, as we have done for welfare mothers.

Funding

The main problem men's programs face is insecure funding. Some federal support for men's work programs is currently available. TANF, the main cash welfare program, is designed mainly to support single-parent families. However, one of its goals is to promote two-parent families, and to this end states are allowed to spend TANF monies on services to noncustodial fathers. This is the basis for TANF-funded men's programs such as NCP Choices. This permission also extends to the contingency funds available under TANF, the emergency TANF funding provided under the stimulus legislation (the American

Recovery and Reinvestment Act, or ARRA) of 2009, and the maintenance-of-effort spending (MOE) states are required to make under TANF.

The following other enactments also provide some support:

- *President's Prison Reentry Initiative,* begun in 2005. Supports faith-based and community organizations helping returning prisoners. Funding is about $20 million a year over 2005–2008.

- *Deficit Reduction Act of 2005,* enacted in 2006. Reauthorized TANF and provides project grants under TANF to fatherhood and marriage programs. The authorization is $150 million a year over 2006–2011.

- *Second Chance Act,* enacted in 2008. Provides funds for demonstration programs in prison reentry. Funding was $15 million in 2009 and 2010.

In his 2011 budget, President Obama proposed to replace the Deficit Reduction Act funding with $500 million in competitive grants for fatherhood and family services.

Further funding may come through fatherhood bills now pending in Congress—the Julia Carson Responsible Fatherhood and Healthy Families Act (HR 2979) in the House and the Responsible Fatherhood and Healthy Families Act (S 1309) in the Senate. Ignoring minor differences, both bills would provide demonstration grants to states for the following:

- *Employment programs* for noncustodial fathers to enable them to pay child support. Funding would be $15 million a year over 2011–15.

- *Transitional jobs programs and "career pathways" partnerships* intended to serve disadvantaged workers, including noncustodial fathers and ex-offenders. Funding would be $35 million a year over 2011–15.

- *Healthy marriage and responsible fatherhood programs.* The $150 million authorization in the Deficit Reduction Act is raised to $200 million through 2015.

This funding, although welcome, falls far short of the $1 billion to $5 billion it would take to serve the 1.2 million men most in need, as estimated above. Just as important, the money has little tie to the mainstream child support and criminal justice systems that must carry out that mission. It goes mostly for one-shot demonstration projects, without staying power, and it goes chiefly to faith-based or other private organizations that apply for the grants. We already know the sort of programs this effort produces— the more voluntary, more service-oriented fatherhood and prison reentry programs surveyed in chapters 3 and 4. Such efforts, though well intentioned, produce little enduring change.

Child Support. Hardly any of my field respondents even mentioned these grants. State child support officials mentioned two other concerns far more prominently. The first was *federal matching of incentive payments.* State CSE programs that perform well receive incentive payments from Washington. States have been accustomed to reinvesting these funds in their child support programs and claiming a 66 percent federal match on them, as they do on state spending for child support. The Deficit Reduction Act forbade this practice to save money, effectively cutting federal funding for CSE. In 2009, ARRA restored matching through 2010 as states wish, but the Obama administration seeks to maintain the cut. Restoring matching permanently would motivate states to spend more of their own money on work programs.

The second concern was *Title IV-D funding.* The strongest complaint I heard in the field is that CSE spending on employment programs is not eligible for matching under Title IV-D of the Social Security Act, the source of federal child support funding. The law is not specific, but to deny matching for employment is the long-standing position of federal authorities. To reverse this ruling—or, if necessary, change the law—would do more than anything else to promote the expansion of men's work programs. The attraction is not only the high federal match—66 percent—but also the fact that Title IV-D is an entitlement, with no definite appropriations limit. Title IV-D access would free states to expand their programs without worrying year to year about funding. It would permit Texas's NCP Choices, which has depended on TANF support, to expand beyond TANF-related cases. It would, as one child support lawyer told me, "change the culture."

The child support provisions of PRWORA actually require that states running TANF provide work programs to which nonpaying fathers with children on TANF can be assigned. But it provides no funding for them, given the current interpretation of Title IV-D. It is time to resolve this contradiction.

Title IV-D funding for work programs might carry the condition, parallel to TANF, that the programs enroll some minimum percentage of the potential clients. Alternatively, states might compete on a performance basis for shares of a fixed appropriation for work programs, although grants would have to cover several years to motivate long-term change.

Criminal Justice. The case for regular federal funding of work programs for prison reentry is weaker. The federal role in criminal justice has always been small, and that system is less ready to change than child support. Here, the existing strategy of demonstration projects has more appeal. The grants should, however, be redirected from community groups to mainstream prison and parole agencies. These are the organizations we want to see running work programs so that they more fully accept the work mission. The agencies, of course, might then contract with the same nongovernmental organizations that are running work programs now.

Evaluation

Besides a lack of secure funding, the main limitation of current policy is insufficient evaluation. Only one work program in child support and one in prison reentry have completed an experimental evaluation. Most other trial efforts, such as the fatherhood programs, escaped impact assessments entirely. Evaluations showing positive impacts are essential before political leaders and administrators will take work programs more seriously. In welfare reform, the early and positive evaluations of work programs done by the Manpower Demonstration Research Corporation in California and other states in the 1980s were essential to launching the movement that finally culminated in PRWORA.

Those studies established that welfare work programs should be mandatory and that ordinary welfare agencies could run them, but they did not resolve all issues. The federal government then funded the elaborate National Evaluation of Welfare-to-Work Strategies (NEWWS). Covering eleven programs over thirteen years (1989–2002), NEWWS aimed mainly to determine whether programs that emphasized training or work first were more effective and whether work tests for mothers would harm children. A clear verdict emerged that work first was best and that children were little affected. The congressional drafters of PRWORA in 1996 had already assumed that a radical, work-first reform was best, but the NEWWS results ratified that judgment.

In men's programs, the role of the early MDRC welfare work studies has been played by PFS, CEO, and the other evaluations surveyed in chapters 3 and 4. These suffice to show that work programs are promising, but they leave some design and administrative issues unresolved, as explained above. Washington should plan a comparative evaluation, akin to NEWWS, that would address those issues. These studies should include cost-benefit calculations because offsets are so important for justifying the budgetary cost of work programs.

A NEWWS-style evaluation is most feasible in the near term in child support because the largest number of serious work programs is likely to develop here. Title IV-D funding would itself cover much of the cost of the studies, as it did in PFS. In criminal justice, as mentioned earlier, programs are likely to be smaller and less stable in the near term. But federal grants for them should still require serious evaluations; even if they were not experimental but based on propensity score matching, as with ComALERT.

The cost of evaluation appears manageable. The PFS study cost $12 million to $15 million, NEWWS about $30 million. But costs in these studies were inflated by the surveys used to track results in PFS and by the NEWWS studies of child and family effects. A study of men's work programs without these dimensions could use unemployment insurance reporting to track employment effects and thus cost much less. The current MDRC assessment of CEO will cost $4 million to $5 million over six or seven years. The Targeted Jobs Reentry Demonstration costs around $5 million. The America Works evaluation will cost only $1 million because it uses private jobs and thus need not pay wages and the other costs of job creation.[1]

The Benefit Side

As suggested in chapter 8, work enforcement for men should be combined with added benefits to "make work pay" more for them than it does now. That means an enhanced wage subsidy paid to low-income workers whether or not they have children to support, but conditional on the recipient working full time and paying his child support judgment, if any.

Existing proposals move in this direction, but without enough conditionality. Gordon Berlin's plan would raise the subsidy rate to 25 percent but require only full-time work (thirty hours a week), not child support payment. The two fatherhood bills now pending would also raise the subsidy, but without stipulations about either work level or payment.

Rather, I would raise the subsidy to 20 or 25 percent but require both full-time work and child support payment in return. I also recommend funding a New Hope–style system of case managers to sell this deal to the men involved. The parent agency might be welfare, child support, or the workforce system. Like child support staff in Milwaukee or Detroit, these staffs would reach out to poor communities, seeking to persuade nonworking men to come in from the cold. The message would be: fulfill your obligations. In return, you will not only avoid trouble but also earn credits to help you become a reliable father to your children. Become a steady worker, and society will help you achieve something in life.

The Need for Vision

One reason welfare reform succeeded is that everyone involved—from senior politicians right down to local staffs—realized that change was crucial to overcoming poverty in America. Those involved in men's programs have generally been less ambitious. Many people I interviewed were lost in the intricacies of child support payment or the parole system. They need to raise their sights. Getting poor men to work more regularly is as vital to rebuilding the inner city as welfare reform and may be more so.

It is time for the child support and criminal justice systems to take on the work problem at a level they have not yet done. National leadership can help to motivate that change. The goal must be to get *all* nonworking men with a work obligation into regular employment or at least enough of them so that voluntary compliance takes over. For low-income men, working regularly must become the norm that it once was. That change alone could break the back of family poverty in America.

To achieve that goal is a political and administrative challenge. Elected leaders must summon the will to do it, and administrators must execute work programs on the ground. Enforcement must grow to the point where men take and hold available jobs on their own. Then, as in welfare, programs could be reduced to the level needed simply to maintain the new expectation. Once again, we will have climbed a mountain and come out on the other side.

Appendix: Method

Much of this study is based on the research of others, especially the evaluations I use to assess programs. Most of my own inquiry is concentrated in chapters 6 and 7. There I analyze whether and how states have implemented work programs for men. This appendix describes in more detail the methods behind those inquiries. The findings are reported in the main text.

The State Survey

To discover how fully states had implemented work programs in the child support of criminal justice systems, my research assistant, Jon Flugstad, and I canvassed all the states during the spring and summer of 2009. I rated the six states where I did fieldwork, and Flugstad rated the others using phone calls to state officials.

Coverage. We obtained results for forty-three out of fifty-one jurisdictions (fifty states plus the District of Columbia). The other states ignored multiple calls, in most cases repeated over more than a month. In child support, the nonresponders included Connecticut, the District of Columbia, Maine, Mississippi, Pennsylvania, Rhode Island, South Carolina, and Utah. In criminal justice, they included Georgia, Hawaii, Idaho, Indiana, Maryland, Nevada, West Virginia, and Wyoming.

Although we could not cover all states, we are confident our results are representative. No state failed to respond to both the child support and criminal justice inquiries, so we have some information on every state. The general character of the men's programs we found was also consistent over the course of the inquiry. It did not change as we moved from the field states to the states that responded to the phone survey quickly and then to the more reluctant states. Also, most of the nonresponders were smaller states; only Pennsylvania ranked in the top ten states in population. Therefore, our results cover the states with the vast bulk of the American population.

Interview Guide. My instructions for the telephone interviewing were as follows:

Call the states that I have not visited (that is, those other than New York, New Jersey, Ohio, Michigan, Texas, and Wisconsin) and determine which are running work programs aimed at low-income men. We are interested in work programs aimed at getting men to work who are already under an obligation to work. That means men who owe child support and must work to pay it and men coming out of prison who are supposed to work as a condition of parole. We want to know which states are running work programs to get *these* men to work more regularly. Thus, we exclude employment programs that are already operating, such as TANF work programs or voluntary employment services under the Workforce Investment Act, as these are not set up specifically for these men. We're interested in steps taken *beyond* these existing programs. In the case of criminal justice, some states—like Michigan—have prison reentry programs with multiple dimensions. We're interested mainly in the work aspects.

In each state, locate the agencies responsible for child support and criminal justice. This means getting real phone numbers for the head administrative office of each state department. Try department web pages, Google, phone book web pages, etc. Respondents should be people senior enough to speak about what a state is doing in men's work programs but not so senior that they are unavailable. That will usually be a deputy secretary/commissioner or possibly a planning/evaluation official. Explain who is running and funding the study.

Ask whether the state has any special programs aimed at getting men owing child support (or, alternatively, parolees) to work more regularly. A program means more than just having regular child support or parole staff refer men to existing programs. There must be a definite program with its own staff that the state is spending money on for the purpose of raising *these* men's work levels. The program, however, may consist of nothing more than special staff to refer men to other agencies. As a guide, see "Child Support and Job Projects for Fathers by State," an Administration for Children and

Families/OCSE listing of state programs as of 2006. If a state is mentioned here, ask specifically about that program.

Key features about the program you need to determine:

- **Is it mandatory?** That is, do men have to participate on pain of some sanctions such as jail or returning to prison? Or can they choose to participate or not without penalty?

- **What is offered?** It might be:

  - *Referral to other programs or agencies,* such as the workforce system, TANF work programs, vocational rehabilitation, etc. The focus must be on work, not other problems such as housing or drug rehabilitation.

  - *Job search.* That is, the program helps/requires men to look for work in the private sector.

  - *Guaranteed jobs.* That is, the program places men in jobs that it creates and pays the men in some manner to do, if only by keeping them out of jail or reducing child support arrears.

  - *Training.* A few programs may offer training in an attempt to get men better jobs, although this is uncommon.

- **Who runs it?** Which agencies are involved? These may include government agencies, contractors, or nonprofits.

- **Who pays for it?** Where does the funding come from? There may be state funds through a particular department or federal funds (e.g., TANF, WIA).

- **How big is it?** Roughly how many men were served at a given time by the program, relative to the potential caseload? A few? A significant minority? A majority? All?

- **Dates.** When did the program begin? If you hear of a program that ended, get the dates of its beginning and end.

If the state claims no programs, ask whether counties or regions within the state are doing anything like this. If so, seek contact information and follow up, although we are principally interested in the state level. Also ask if respondents know of comparable programs in other states—this is to get leads for further calls.

Field Interviews

I interviewed state and local officials in six states in order to obtain a better sense of how they viewed the men's work problem and why they had or had not undertaken major initiatives to address it. The focus was on how the states defined the problem and the factors governing the initiation and implementation of men's work programs.

Coverage. I needed to choose states that would help me answer these questions and, at the same time, be representative of the nation. At the outset, neither I nor others I consulted had a good sense of which states were prominent in men's programming. So I proceeded incrementally, interviewing first in states where I had contacts from previous research—New Jersey, New York, and Wisconsin. In these states, I could also get permission to interview. Clearance was a significant problem. Child support and criminal justice agencies are much less accustomed to research inquiries than welfare agencies are (due to welfare reform). Some were suspicious of my questions, especially in criminal justice. One prison agency refused me all entry. Fortunately, enough other agencies in that state cooperated, so I could still get the information I needed.

It turned out that none of these early states was a significant innovator in men's work programs. But I heard of others that were—Michigan, Ohio, and Texas—and went there. Fortunately, these later states also complemented the early ones in other respects. I emerged with six states that covered a wide range in terms of region and political tradition as well as innovation in the area of men's work programs.

General Approach. As with the state survey, my interviews were based on an interview guide rather than a fixed survey instrument. That is, I had a list of topics that I attempted to cover in each interview; I did not use scripted language, as pollsters do. Rather, I carried on a conversation with respondents that covered my areas of interest.

This interviewing was much more open ended and less structured than that used in the state survey. These were my practices in the following areas, based on long experience in this kind of research:

- *Planning.* Think through the interview guide carefully. Choose topics that address your research question and your initial hypotheses—in this case whether and how states might innovate in the area of men's work programs.

- *Sampling.* Distribute your respondents around the organization you are studying, including people in different positions and junior as well as senior people.

- *Confidentiality.* Think through how much confidentiality to offer respondents. Confidentiality is most needed when questions are sensitive and respondents are junior. In this case, I did not explicitly promise confidentiality because the questions were not particularly sensitive and most of my interlocutors were used to dealing with these issues. However, other than the most senior respondents, I did not identify respondents by name in my write-up.

- *Record responses.* Taping allows a verbatim transcript, but it is costly to transcribe. Taking notes is less off-putting to respond ents, but you can write down only short quotations. I have preferred notes to economize on time and to promote candor.

- *Establishing rapport:* At the start of the interview, chat in a friendly way with the respondents to establish that you know the jargon and acronyms of the field. The respondents should realize that they will not have to educate you about the basics. Rather, they can talk candidly about issues in which you have a mutual interest.

- *Describing your agenda.* Keep it general. Specify the subject you are working on, but not all the details of the project or your own views or hypotheses. Do not mention your own point of view, if you have one, lest it bias what people say.

- *Order of questions.* Tackle subjects as they come up. You need not cover your list of subjects completely or in a set order. Rather, get respondents talking about the general subject and then steer the conversation around to the specific topics.

- *Neutrality.* Avoid questions that are leading, that presume an answer, or that have a critical or evaluative edge to them. Such questions may bias what people say. Pose issues so as to leave a real choice. Don't make respondents think you're assessing them.

- *The general and the specific.* On any subject, begin with broad, open-ended questions and move to more specific ones. Get the respondents talking in their own terms about the subject. Then follow up with narrower questions to nail down details.

- *Getting the facts.* Ask for description, not analysis or evaluation. Ask respondents to describe what they do, or the operations of the organization. Get the facts about what happens as a reporter would—who did what, when, and how. Assessment is secondary and can get in the way. Only at the end of the interview, with the facts in the can, should you step back and ask more evaluative questions.

- *Serendipity.* If unexpected findings emerge, revise your interview guide and pursue them. Likewise, eliminate questions that prove to be meaningless or elicit nothing.

Interview Guide. The following was my interview guide for the men's work project:

- What is your current position in this agency? How long have you been with the agency? In what positions?

- My project is about how to improve work levels among low-income men. When I mention the employment problem among low-income men, what do you think of?

  - *Unemployment, lack of employment?*

  - *Irregular work, where men get jobs but lose them?*

- *Low wages? Low skills?*

- *Decline in labor force participation?*

- What causes the problem?

  - *In general, work levels in American society are high—higher than in most other rich countries. Yet we find low-income men generally don't work regularly. Only about 40 percent of poor men work at all in a year—even when the economy is booming. Why is that?*

- What is your agency doing about this?

  - *Work policies of any kind?*

  - *Work programs?*

  - *Any evaluations?*

- How important is the work problem alongside other goals you have?

  - *In child support: compared to collecting support.*

  - *In criminal justice: compared to incarcerating offenders and protecting public safety.*

  - *Traditionally, these agencies typically did not focus on work. Why not?*

- What would be the ideal solution?

  - *Suppose you could do anything you wanted to solve the problem, what would it be?*

- The current thinking in Washington is that we may need special work programs designed for poor men with employment problems. There have been experimental work programs:

  - *In child support—Parents' Fair Share, various fatherhood programs.*

  - *In criminal justice—prison reentry programs, the Center for Employment Opportunities, Ready4Work.*

  - *What have you heard about these programs?*

- Evaluations suggest they have some potential to reduce nonwork among their clients. How about a national work program to serve two groups?

  - *Men who are behind on their child support due to employment problems.*

  - *Ex-offenders leaving the prisons on parole.*

- What is your view of work programs like this?

  - *A good idea? A waste of money?*

  - *Should work programs be mandatory?*

  - *The problem is that men don't come forward for programs, or they drop out. How do you get a grip on these guys?*

  - *Should programs focus on work first or on training?*

- Right now, these programs are only small and experimental.

  - *Could they be taken to scale?*

  - *Could a program serve all parolees and child support defaulters with work problems?*

- What would be the problems with doing this?

  - *Cost?*

  - *Administration?*

  - *Politics?*

I did not cover all of these topics with every respondent. Rather, I covered what each speaker knew the most about or wanted to talk about. I also varied the questions as I learned more in a given state, omitting those that had been answered sufficiently and adding others that arose in the field. The approach was similar to that of a journalist—pursuing topics of interest down to greater detail. But unlike most journalism, there was an analytic structure in the background derived from prior research, my own and others'.

Data Analysis. A major challenge in fieldwork is handling the immense complexity you encounter. Social programs and their implementation are always surrounded with myriad details, too many to report. There is simply more information out there than is found in any quantitative database. My method has been to (1) review my notes from respondents right after the interviews, sometimes calling or e-mailing them for clarifications; (2) write a summary in my own words of what I had heard from each respondent, the state as a whole, or both; and (3) report the findings in my write-up, in this case in chapter 7. At each stage there is progressively less detail and more focus on addressing the questions that motivated the inquiry in the first place. Typically, the field summaries are the main basis for the write-up.

Notes

Introduction

1. U.S. Census Bureau, March Current Population Survey for 1994 (table 19) and 2000 (table 17). Figures add to over 100 percent because Hispanics are an ethnic category that overlaps the racial categories.

2. Various studies weight welfare reform, the economy, and the earned income tax credit (EITC) differently in explaining the caseload fall. I credit welfare reform most heavily because it was the sharpest change from the 1980s, when the economy was also good but did not generate caseload fall. And although statistical studies credit the EITC, most welfare officials I have talked to in New York City and Wisconsin say it had little or no influence. I think higher work levels drove up EITC, rather than vice versa, as the studies assume.

3. I have documented these shifts in the debate in Lawrence M. Mead, "Welfare Politics in Congress: An Analysis of Hearings, 1962–1996" (New York University, Department of Politics, April 2010).

4. Blaine Harden, "'Dead Broke' Dads' Child Support Struggle," *New York Times,* January 29, 2002, A19; and Erik Eckholm, "Help for the Hardest Part of Prison: Staying Out," *New York Times,* August 12, 2006, A1, A12.

Chapter 1: Poor Men's Work Programs

1. Calculated from U.S. Census Bureau, *Current Population Survey* (March 2010).

2. Harry J. Holzer, Paul Offner, and Elaine Sorensen, "Declining Employment among Young Black Less-Educated Men: The Role of Incarceration and Child Support," *Journal of Policy Analysis and Management* 24, no. 2 (Spring 2005): 330–33.

3. William Julius Wilson, *When Work Disappears: The World of the New Urban Poor* (New York: Knopf, 1996).

4. Jason DeParle, "Raising Kevion," *New York Times,* August 22, 2004, 26–31ff.

5. Kathryn Edin and Maria Kefalas, *Promises I Can Keep: Why Poor Women Put Motherhood before Marriage* (Berkeley: University of California Press, 2005), chaps. 2–3.

6. U.S. Department of Labor, Office of Policy Planning and Research, *The Negro Family: The Case for National Action* ["Moynihan Report"] (Washington, DC:

Government Printing Office, March 1965), chap. 2; U.S. Department of Health and Human Services, National Center for Health Statistics, *Health, United States, 2009: With Special Feature on Medical Technology* (Hyattsville, MD: National Center for Health Statistics, 2010), table 9.

7. Crime rate data from U.S. Department of Justice, Bureau of Justice Statistics; Heather C. West and William J. Sabol, "Prison Inmates at Midyear 2008—Statistical Tables," U.S. Department of Justice, Bureau of Justice Statistics, March 2009, table 15.

8. Jeremy Travis, *But They All Come Back: Facing the Challenges of Prison Reentry* (Washington, DC: Urban Institute Press, 2005), 164.

9. Edin and Kefalas, *Promises I Can Keep,* chaps. 2–3.

10. Travis, *But They All Come Back,* 167–68; Joan Petersilia, *When Prisoners Come Home: Parole and Prisoner Reentry* (Oxford: Oxford University Press, 2003), 112; Christopher Uggen, "Work as a Turning Point in the Life Course of Criminals: A Duration Model of Age, Employment, and Recidivism," *American Sociological Review* 65, no. 4 (August 2000): 529–46.

11. West and Sabol, "Prison Inmates at Midyear 2008," table 16.

12. Peter Edelman, Harry J. Holzer, and Paul Offner, *Reconnecting Disadvantaged Young Men* (Washington, DC: Urban Institute Press, 2006), 25.

13. Arland Thornton and Linda Young-DeMarco, "Four Decades of Trends in Attitudes toward Family Issues in the United States: The 1960s through the 1990s," *Journal of Marriage and Family* 63, no. 4 (November 2001): 1009–37.

14. Ronald B. Mincy, "What about Black Fathers?" *The American Prospect,* April 8, 2002, 56–58.

15. Martin Gilens, *Why Americans Hate Welfare: Race, Media, and the Politics of Antipoverty Policy* (Chicago: University of Chicago Press, 1999), chaps. 2, 8.

16. U.S. Census Bureau, *Current Population Survey,* Child Support Supplement, April 2008, table 4.

17. William Sabol, Heather C. West, and Matthew Cooper, "Prisoners in 2008," U.S. Department of Justice, Bureau of Justice Statistics, December 2009, table 3; Lauren E. Glaze and Thomas P. Bonczar, "Probation and Parole in the United States, 2008," U.S. Department of Justice, Bureau of Justice Statistics, December 2009, tables 1 and 4.

18. Travis, *But They All Come Back,* 162–63.

19. This is consistent with Bruce Western's estimate, citing other sources, that "one-half to three-quarters" of released prisoners are out of work in their first months after release. See Bruce Western, *From Prison to Work: A Proposal for a National Prisoner Reentry Program* (Washington, DC: Brookings, December 2008), 17.

20. Holzer, Offner, and Sorensen, "Declining Employment," 334 n10.

Chapter 2: Causes of Nonwork

1. Much of this chapter follows Lawrence M. Mead, "Toward a Mandatory Work Policy for Men," *The Future of Children* 17, no. 2 (September 2007): 46–55.

NOTES TO PAGES 15–17   129

2. The estimates come from Chinhui Juhn, Kevin M. Murphy, and Robert H. Topel, "Why Has the Natural Rate of Unemployment Increased over Time?" *Brookings Papers on Economic Activity*, no. 2 (1991): 75–142; Lawrence F. Katz, "Wage Subsidies for the Disadvantaged," in *Generating Jobs: How to Increase Demand for Less-Skilled Workers*, ed. Richard B. Freeman and Peter Gottschalk (New York: Russell Sage, 1998), chap. 1; and Jeff Grogger, "Market Wages and Youth Crime," *Journal of Labor Economics* 16, no. 4 (October 1998): 756–91. My thanks to Harry Holzer for these sources.

3. Harry J. Holzer and Paul Offner, "Trends in the Employment Outcomes of Young Black Men, 1979–2000," in *Black Males Left Behind*, ed. Ronald B. Mincy (Washington, DC: Urban Institute Press, 2006), chap. 2.

4. Ronald F. Ferguson, "The Working-Poverty Trap," *The Public Interest*, no. 158 (Winter 2005): 71–82.

5. George J. Borjas, "The Demographic Determinants of the Demand for Black Labor," in *The Black Youth Employment Crisis*, ed. Richard B. Freeman and Harry J. Holzer (Chicago: University of Chicago Press, 1986), chap. 5; Rebecca M. Blank and Jonah Gelbach, "Are Less-Educated Women Crowding Less-Educated Men Out of the Labor Market?" in *Black Males Left Behind*, ed. Mincy, chap. 5.

6. George J. Borjas, *Heaven's Door: Immigration Policy and the American Economy* (Princeton, NJ: Princeton University Press, 1999), chap. 4; George J. Borjas, "The Labor Demand Curve Is Downward Sloping: Reexamining the Impact of Immigration on the Labor Market," *Quarterly Journal of Economics* 118, no. 4 (November 2003): 1335–74. For the debate about the issue, see Roger Lowenstein, "The Immigration Equation," *New York Times Magazine*, July 9, 2006, 36–43, 69–71.

7. Elijah Anderson, *Streetwise: Race, Class, and Change in an Urban Community* (Chicago: University of Chicago Press, 1990), chap. 3; Elijah Anderson, *Code of the Street: Decency, Violence, and the Moral Life of the Inner City* (New York: Norton, 1999), chap. 3. Anderson does not suggest that all employment is unavailable to poor youth, nor do his findings support this.

8. Steven D. Levitt and Sudhir Alladi Venkatesh, "An Economic Analysis of a Drug-Selling Gang's Finances," *Quarterly Journal of Economics* 115, no. 3 (August 2000): 755–89. My thanks to Peter Reuter for helping me interpret this research.

9. William Julius Wilson, *When Work Disappears: The World of the New Urban Poor* (New York: Knopf, 1996); William Julius Wilson, *The Truly Disadvantaged: The Inner City, the Underclass, and Public Policy* (Chicago: University of Chicago Press, 1987).

10. Peter Edelman, Harry J. Holzer, and Paul Offner, *Reconnecting Disadvantaged Young Men* (Washington, DC: Urban Institute Press, 2006), 28–30.

11. Holzer and Offner, "Trends in the Employment Outcomes," 24.

12. Harry J. Holzer, Paul Offner, and Elaine Sorensen, "Declining Employment among Young Black Less-Educated Men: The Role of Incarceration and Child Support," *Journal of Policy Analysis and Management* 24, no. 2 (Spring 2005): 333–47. My thanks to Harry Holzer for helping me interpret these trends.

13. Frank E. Furstenberg Jr., Kay E. Sherwood, and Mercer L. Sullivan, *Caring and Paying: What Fathers and Mothers Say about Child Support* (New York: Manpower Demonstration Research Corporation, July 1992); Dan Bloom and Kay Sherwood, *Matching Opportunities to Obligations: Lessons for Child Support Reform from the Parents' Fair Share Pilot Phase* (New York: Manpower Demonstration Research Corporation, April 1994), chap. 3; Kathryn Edin and Maria Kefalas, *Promises I Can Keep: Why Poor Women Put Motherhood before Marriage* (Berkeley: University of California Press, 2005). Some ethnographers still believe that structural barriers, such as jobs mismatch, deny the poor the chance to work. But their own findings, in my view, belie these claims.

14. Lawrence M. Mead, *The New Politics of Poverty: The Nonworking Poor in America* (New York: Basic Books, 1992), chap. 7.

15. Elijah Anderson, "The Story of John Turner," *The Public Interest,* no. 108 (Summer 1992): 3–34; Mark Kleiman, "Coerced Abstinence: A Neopaternalist Drug Policy Initiative," in *The New Paternalism: Supervisory Approaches to Poverty,* ed. Lawrence M. Mead (Washington, DC: Brookings, 1997), chap. 6.

16. Anderson, *Streetwise,* 242–43; Anderson, *Code of the Street,* 36; Orlando Patterson, "A Poverty of the Mind," *New York Times,* March 26, 2006, 13.

17. Elliot Liebow, *Tally's Corner: A Study of Negro Streetcorner Men* (Boston: Little, Brown, 1967).

18. Harry Eckstein, "Civic Inclusion and Its Discontents," *Daedalus* 113, no. 4 (Fall 1984): 107–45.

19. Philippe I. Bourgois, *In Search of Respect: Selling Crack in El Barrio,* 2nd ed. (Cambridge: Cambridge University Press, 2003); Ken Auletta, *The Underclass* (New York: Random House, 1982), 158–74.

20. Lawrence M. Mead, *Government Matters: Welfare Reform in Wisconsin* (Princeton, NJ: Princeton University Press, 2004), chap. 8.

21. Harry J. Holzer, "Black Youth Nonemployment: Duration and Job Search," in *Black Youth Employment Crisis,* ed. Freeman and Holzer, chap. 1.

22. Anderson, *Code of the Street,* chap. 3; Alford A. Young, "Low-Income Black Men on Work Opportunity, Work Resources, and Job Training Programs," in *Black Males Left Behind,* ed. Mincy, 150–58.

23. Joleen Kirschenman and Kathryn M. Neckerman, "'We'd Love to Hire Them, But . . .': The Meaning of Race for Employers," in *The Urban Underclass,* ed. Christopher Jencks and Paul E. Peterson (Washington, DC: Brookings, 1991), 203–32.

24. Anderson, *Code of the Street,* chap. 5.

25. Harvey C. Mansfield, *Manliness* (New Haven, CT: Yale University Press, 2006); Francis Fukuyama, *The End of History and the Last Man* (New York: Free Press, 1992), chaps. 13–19.

26. Anderson, *Streetwise,* chap. 6.

27. Ibid., chap. 3; Anderson, *Code of the Street,* chaps. 2–3; Bourgois, *In Search of Respect.*

28. Anderson, *Streetwise,* chap. 4; Anderson, *Code of the Street,* chap. 4.

29. Mary Achatz and Crystal A. MacAllum, *Young Unwed Fathers: Report from the Field* (Philadelphia: Public/Private Ventures, Spring 1994), 89–91.

30. Edin and Kefalas, *Promises I Can Keep,* 135–36, 177–79.

31. Sean Joe, "Suicide Patterns among Black Males," in *Against the Wall: Poor, Young, Black, and Male,* ed. Elijah Anderson (Philadelphia: University of Pennsylvania Press, 2008), chap. 14.

32. Edin and Kefalas, *Promises I Can Keep,* chaps. 2–4.

33. Anderson, *Code of the Street,* chaps. 4–5; Liebow, *Tally's Corner,* chaps. 2–4.

34. Avner Ahituv and Robert I. Lerman, "How Do Marital Status, Work Effort, and Wage Rates Interact?" *Demography* 44, no. 3 (August 2007): 623–47.

35. Ronald Mincy, Jennifer Hill, and Marilyn Sinkewicz, "Marriage: Cause or Mere Indicator of Future Earnings Growth?" *Journal of Policy Analysis and Management* 28, no. 3 (Summer 2009): 417–39.

36. See notes 32 and 33.

37. Liebow, *Tally's Corner,* 15–16.

38. I credit this view to Lorraine C. Blackman, a professor of social work at Indiana University.

39. Daniel P. Moynihan, "A Family Policy for the Nation," *America,* September 18, 1965, 283.

40. Mead, *New Politics of Poverty,* chaps. 4–6.

41. Edelman, Holzer, and Offner, *Reconnecting Disadvantaged Young Men,* 24.

42. Mead, *New Politics of Poverty,* 147–55.

43. U.S. Department of Labor web page (accessed February 1, 2010).

44. I ignore here the temporary enhancements of EITC legislated as part of the 2009 American Recovery and Reinvestment Act.

45. Robert Moffitt, "Incentive Effects of the U.S. Welfare System: A Review," *Journal of Economic Literature* 30, no. 1 (March 1992): 13–19.

46. Bruce D. Meyer and Dan T. Rosenbaum, "Welfare, the Earned Income Tax Credit, and the Labor Supply of Single Mothers," *Quarterly Journal of Economics* 116, no. 3 (August 2001): 1063–1114; Jeffrey Grogger, "The Effects of Time Limits, the EITC, and Other Policy Changes on Welfare Use, Work, and Income among Female-Headed Families," *Review of Economics and Statistics* 85, no. 2 (May 2003): 394–408. See Introduction, n. 2.

47. Gary Burtless, "The Work Response to a Guaranteed Income: A Survey of Experimental Evidence," in *Lessons from the Income Maintenance Experiments: Proceedings of a Conference Held in September 1986,* ed. Alicia H. Munnell (Boston: Federal Reserve Bank of Boston, n.d.), 22–52. Burtless concludes that "the labor supply functions estimated in the experiments are vertical or backward-bending" (48).

48. Greg J. Duncan, Aletha C. Huston, and Thomas S. Weisner, *Higher Ground: New Hope for the Working Poor and Their Children* (New York: Russell Sage Foundation, 2007), 62–63.

49. Howard S. Bloom, James A. Riccio, and Nandita Verma, *Promoting Work in Public Housing: The Effectiveness of JOBS-Plus: Final Report* (New York: MDRC, March 2005), chap. 4.

50. Ronald Ferguson and Randall Filer, "Do Better Jobs Make Better Workers? Absenteeism from Work among Inner-City Black Youths," in *Black Youth Employment Crisis*, ed. Freeman and Holzer, chap. 7; Christopher Uggen and Jeremy Staff, "Work as a Turning Point for Criminal Offenders," *Corrections Management Quarterly* 5, no. 4 (September 2001): 8–10, 13.

51. These include Big Brothers Big Sisters, Children's Aid Society–Carrera, and the Quantum Opportunities Program.

52. Here and below I rely heavily on Robert Lerman, *Helping Out-of-School Youth Attain Labor Market Success: What We Know and How to Learn More* (Washington, DC: Urban Institute, 2005); and Robert Lerman, "Are Skills the Problem?" in *A Future of Good Jobs? America's Challenge in the Global Economy,* ed. Timothy J. Bartik and Susan N. Houseman (Kalamazoo, MI: Upjohn, 2008), chap. 2.

53. Larry L. Orr, Howard S. Bloom, Stephen H. Bell, Fred Doolittle, Winston Lin, and George Cave, *Does Training for the Disadvantaged Work? Evidence from the National JTPA Study* (Washington, DC: Urban Institute, 1996), chap. 4. All the estimates I mention were too small to be statistically significant at usual levels.

54. Robert J. LaLonde, "The Promise of Public Sector–Sponsored Training Programs," *Journal of Economic Perspectives* 9, no. 2 (Spring 1995): 149–68.

55. James J. Heckman, "Doing It Right: Job Training and Education," *The Public Interest,* no. 135 (Spring 1999): 86–107.

56. Lloyd Ulman, "The Uses and Limits of Manpower Policy," *The Public Interest,* no. 34 (Winter 1974): 97–98.

57. Lawrence M. Mead, "Welfare Employment," in *New Paternalism,* ed. Mead, chap. 2; Mead, *Government Matters,* chap. 8.

58. Chester E. Finn Jr., "Paternalism Goes to School," in *New Paternalism,* ed. Mead, chap. 7; David Whitman, *Sweating the Small Stuff: Inner-City Schools and the New Paternalism* (Washington, DC: Thomas B. Fordham Institute, 2008).

59. James J. Kemple, *Career Academies: Long-Term Impacts on Labor Market Outcomes, Educational Attainment, and Transitions to Adulthood* (New York: MDRC, June 2008).

60. Peter Z. Schochet, John Burghardt, and Sheena McConnell, "Does Job Corps Work? Impact Findings from the National Job Corps Study," *American Economic Review* 98, no. 5 (December 2008): 1864–86.

61. Lerman, "Helping Out-of-School Youth," 22–24.

62. Bloom and Sherwood, *Matching Opportunities to Obligations,* 152–54.

63. Hugh Price, foreword, in Edelman, Holzer, and Offner, *Reconnecting Disadvantaged Young Men,* xiv–xv.

64. U.S. Department of Labor, Office of Policy Planning and Research, *The Negro Family: The Case for National Action* ["Moynihan Report"] (Washington, DC: Government Printing Office, March 1965), 16, 40–43.

65. Joshua D. Angrist, "Estimating the Labor Market Impact of Voluntary Military Service Using Social Security Data on Military Applicants," *Econometrica* 66, no. 2 (March 1998): 249–88; Meredith A. Kleykamp, "College, Jobs, or the Military? Enlistment during a Time of War," *Social Science Quarterly* 87, no. 2 (June 2006): 272–90; Meredith A. Kleykamp, *A Great Place to Start? The Effect of Prior Military Service on Hiring* (Lawrence, KS: University of Kansas, Department of Sociology, February 2007).

66. Hugh B. Price, *Demilitarizing What the Pentagon Knows About Developing Young People: A New Paradigm for Educating Students Who Are Struggling in School and in Life* (Washington, DC: Brookings, May 2007).

67. Dan Bloom, Alissa Gardenhire-Crooks, and Conrad Mandsager, *Reengaging High School Dropouts: Early Results of the National Guard ChalleNGe Program Evaluation* (New York: MDRC, February 2009); Megan Millenky, Dan Bloom, and Colleen Dillon, *Making the Transition: Interim Results of the National Guard Youth ChalleNGe Evaluation* (New York: MDRC, May 2010).

68. Oliver Sloman, *Imagining Nonmilitary Public Schools in the Image of Public Military Academies* (New York: Goldman Sachs Foundation and Taconic Foundation, October 1, 2008).

69. Thomas J. Kane, "Giving Back Control: Long-Term Poverty and Motivation," *Social Service Review* 61, no. 3 (September 1987): 405–19.

70. Schochet, Burghardt, and McConnell, "Does Job Corps Work?" 1875–77; Christopher Uggen, "Work as a Turning Point in the Life Course of Criminals: A Duration Model of Age, Employment, and Recidivism," *American Sociological Review* 65, no. 4 (August 2000): 529–46; Uggen and Staff, "Work as a Turning Point for Criminal Offenders."

Chapter 3: Child Support Enforcement

1. Lawrence M. Mead, "Welfare Caseload Change: An Alternative Approach," *Policy Studies Journal* 31, no. 2 (May 2003): 163–85.

2. U.S. Congress, House Committee on Ways and Means, *2008 Green Book: Background Material, and Data on the Programs within the Jurisdiction of the Committee on Ways and Means* (Washington, DC: Government Printing Office, 2008), 8.78–8.79.

3. Chien-Chang Huang, James Kunz, and Irwin Garfinkel, "The Effect of Child Support on Welfare Exits and Re-Entries," *Journal of Policy Analysis and Management* 21, no. 4 (Fall 2002): 557–76.

4. The following account draws on Dan Bloom and Kay Sherwood, *Matching Opportunities to Obligations: Lessons for Child Support Reform from the Parents' Fair Share Pilot Phase* (New York: Manpower Demonstration Research Corporation, April 1994); Jocelyn Elise Crowley, *The Politics of Child Support in America* (Cambridge: Cambridge University Press, 2003); Jocelyn Elise Crowley, "Supervised Devolution: The Case of Child-Support Enforcement," *Publius* 30, nos. 1–2 (Winter/Spring 2000): 99–117;

Irwin Garfinkel, *Assuring Child Support: An Extension of Social Security* (New York: Russell Sage Foundation, 1992); Jyl J. Josephson, *Gender, Families, and State: Child Support Policy in the United States* (Lanham, MD: Rowman and Littlefield, 1997); Maureen A. Pirog and Kathleen M. Ziol-Guest, "Child Support Enforcement: Programs and Policies, Impacts, and Questions," *Journal of Policy Analysis and Management* 25, no. 4 (Fall 2006): 943–90; Ronald B. Mincy and Hillard Pouncy, "Paternalism, Child Support Enforcement, and Fragile Families," in *The New Paternalism: Supervisory Approaches to Poverty,* ed. Lawrence M. Mead (Washington, DC: Brookings, 1997), chap. 4; and U.S. Congress, *2008 Green Book,* section 8.

5. U.S. Congress, *2008 Green Book,* 8.71–8.77.

6. Lawrence M. Mead, *Government Matters: Welfare Reform in Wisconsin* (Princeton, NJ: Princeton University Press, 2004), 162.

7. Bloom and Sherwood, *Matching Opportunities to Obligations,* 87–88; Fred Doolittle, Virginia Knox, Cynthia Miller, and Sharon Rowser, *Building Opportunities, Enforcing Obligations: Implementation and Interim Impacts of Parents' Fair Share* (New York: Manpower Demonstration Research Corporation, December 1998), 92–94.

8. Elaine Sorensen, "Child Support Gains Some Ground" (Washington, DC: Urban Institute, October 6, 2003).

9. U.S. Office of Child Support Enforcement, *FY 2005 Annual Report to Congress* (Washington, DC: U.S. Department of Health and Human Services, Administration for Children and Families, May 2008), 15.

10. George Gilder, *Visible Man: A True Story of Post-Racist America* (New York: Basic Books, 1978); and Charles Murray, *Losing Ground: American Social Policy, 1950–1980* (New York: Basic Books, 1984).

11. Maureen B. Waller and Robert Plotnick, "Effective Child Support Policy for Low-Income Families: Evidence from Street Level Research," *Journal of Policy Analysis and Management* 20, no. 1 (Winter 2001): 89–110.

12. Maria Cancian, Daniel R. Meyer, and Emma Caspar, "Welfare and Child Support: Complements, Not Substitutes," *Journal of Policy Analysis and Management* 27, no. 2 (Spring 2008): 354–75.

13. Ronald B. Mincy and Elaine J. Sorensen, "Deadbeats and Turnips in Child Support Reform," *Journal of Policy Analysis and Management* 17, no. 1 (Winter 1998): 44–51.

14. Waller and Plotnick, "Effective Child Support Policy."

15. Frank E. Furstenberg Jr., Kay E. Sherwood, and Mercer L. Sullivan, *Caring and Paying: What Fathers and Mothers Say about Child Support* (New York: Manpower Demonstration Research Corporation, July 1992); Earl S. Johnson and Fred Doolittle, "Low-Income Parents and the Parents' Fair Share Demonstration" (New York: Manpower Demonstration Research Corporation, June 1996).

16. Kay S. Hymowitz, "Dads in the 'Hood,'" *City Journal* 14, no. 2 (Autumn 2004): 47.

17. Fred Doolittle and Suzanne Lynn, *Working with Low-Income Cases: Lessons for the Child Support Enforcement System from Parents' Fair Share* (New York: Manpower Demonstration Research Corporation, May 1998), 37.

18. Mead, *Government Matters,* 161–64.

19. Daniel Schroeder and Nicholas Doughty, *Texas Non-Custodial Parent Choices: Program Impact Analysis* (Austin: University of Texas at Austin, Lyndon B. Johnson School of Public Affairs, August 2009), 39; personal communications from Michael Hayes, Office of the Attorney General, February 2009 and October 2010. The 522,689 include both paying and nonpaying cases.

20. Doolittle et al., *Building Opportunities, Enforcing Obligations,* 25–36.

21. Bloom and Sherwood, *Matching Opportunities to Obligations,* chaps. 3, 5; Furstenberg, Sherwood, and Sullivan, *Caring and Paying*; Johnson and Doolittle, "Low-Income Parents."

22. Crowley, *Politics of Child Support,* chaps. 4–7.

23. The information on these programs is based mainly on Karin Martinson and Demetra Nightingale, "Ten Key Findings from Responsible Fatherhood Initiatives" (Washington, DC: Urban Institute, February 2008).

24. Ibid.; Mary Achatz and Crystal A. MacAllum, *Young Unwed Fathers: Report from the Field* (Philadelphia: Public/Private Ventures, Spring 1994), 6; Karin Martinson, John Trutko, Demetra Smith Nightingale, Pamela A. Holcomb, and Burt S. Barnowet, *The Implementation of the Partners for Fragile Families Demonstration Projects* (Washington, DC: Urban Institute, June 2007), 16, 23–24.

25. The information on these results is based on Doolittle et al., *Building Opportunities, Enforcing Obligations,* chaps. 3, 6; John M. Martinez and Cynthia Miller, *Working and Earning: The Impact of Parents' Fair Share on Low-Income Fathers' Employment* (New York: Manpower Demonstration Research Corporation, October 2000), 21–36; Virginia Knox and Cindy Redcross, *Parenting and Providing: The Impact of Parents' Fair Share on Paternal Involvement* (New York: Manpower Demonstration Research Corporation, October 2000), 35–53.

26. Cynthia Miller and Virginia Knox, *The Challenge of Helping Low-Income Fathers Support Their Children: Final Lessons from Parents' Fair Share* (New York: Manpower Demonstration Research Corporation, November 2001), 12–16.

27. Ron Blasco, *Children First Program: Final Evaluation Report* (Madison, WI: Department of Workforce Development, November 2000).

28. Schroeder and Doughty, "Texas Non-Custodial Parent Choices," 44–71.

29. Debra G. Klinman and Joelle H. Sander, *The Teen Parent Collaboration: Reaching and Serving the Teenage Father* (New York: Bank Street College of Education, September 1985), 59.

30. Achatz and MacAllum, *Young Unwed Fathers,* 59–60, 68–70.

31. Jessica Pearson, Nancy Thoennes, Jane Venohr, and David Price, *OCSE Responsible Fatherhood Programs: Client Characteristics and Program Outcomes* (Denver: Center for Policy Research and Policy Studies, September 2003), 156–72.

32. Thomas M. Fraker, Dan M. Levy, Irma Perez-Johnson, Alan M. Hershey, Demetra S. Nightingale, Robert B. Olsen, and Rita A. Stapulonis, *The National Evaluation of the Welfare-to-Work Grants Program: Final Report* (Washington, DC: Mathematica Policy

Research, September 2004), xvi–xvii. The only evaluated local program that served mainly men was in Milwaukee.

33. Karin Martinson, Demetra Smith Nightingale, Pamela A. Holcomb, Burt S. Barnow, and John Trutko, *Partners for Fragile Families Demonstration Projects: Employment and Child Support Outcomes and Trends* (Washington, DC: Urban Institute, September 2007), 7–17.

34. Mincy and Pouncy, "Paternalism, Child Support Enforcement, and Fragile Families," 137–55.

Chapter 4: Criminal Justice

1. William Sabol, Heather C. West, and Matthew Cooper, "Prisoners in 2008," U.S. Department of Justice, Bureau of Justice Statistics, December 2009, table 3.

2. Patrick A. Langan and David J. Levin, "Recidivism of Prisoners Released in 1994," U.S. Department of Justice, Bureau of Justice Statistics, June 2002.

3. Robert Martinson, "What Works? Questions and Answers about Prison Reform," *The Public Interest*, no. 35 (Spring 1974): 22–54.

4. Joan Petersilia, *When Prisoners Come Home: Parole and Prisoner Reentry* (Oxford: Oxford University Press, 2003), 175–84, 246–47; Jeremy Travis, *But They All Come Back: Facing the Challenges of Prison Reentry* (Washington, DC: Urban Institute Press, 2005), 107–8, 168–71.

5. David B. Wilson, Catherine A. Gallagher, and Doris L. MacKenzie, "A Meta-Analysis of Corrections-Based Education, Vocation, and Work Programs for Adult Offenders," *Journal of Research in Crime and Delinquency* 37, no. 4 (November 2000): 347–68; and David Farabee, *Rethinking Rehabilitation: Why Can't We Reform Our Criminals?* (Washington, DC: AEI Press, 2005).

6. Petersilia, *When Prisoners Come Home,* chap. 4; Travis, *But They All Come Back,* chap. 3.

7. Amy L. Solomon, Vera Kachnowski, and Avinash Bhati, *Does Parole Work? Analyzing the Impact of Postprison Supervision on Rearrest Outcomes* (Washington, DC: Urban Institute, March 2005).

8. Joan Petersilia and Susan Turner, "Intensive Probation and Parole," *Criminal Justice: A Review of Research* 17 (1993): 281–335.

9. Petersilia, *When Prisoners Come Home,* 84.

10. Ibid., 55–75; Joan Petersilia, "When Prisoners Return to the Community: Political, Economic, and Social Consequences," *Corrections Management Quarterly* 5, no. 3 (June 2001): 1–10.

11. Martinson, "What Works," 49–50; Marc F. Plattner, "The Rehabilitation of Punishment," *The Public Interest*, no. 44 (Summer 1976): 104–14; James Q. Wilson, *Thinking about Crime* (New York: Vintage, 1977), chaps. 8, 10.

12. Chris Suellentrop, "The Right Has a Jailhouse Conversion: How Conservatives Came to Embrace Prison Reform," *New York Times Magazine,* December 24, 2006, 46–51; "A Nation of Jailbirds," *Economist,* April 4, 2009, 40.

13. Martin Horn, "Rethinking Sentences," *Corrections Management Quarterly* 5, no. 3 (June 2001): 34–40.

14. James Q. Wilson and George L. Kelling Jr., "Broken Windows: The Police and Neighborhood Safety," *Atlantic Monthly,* March 1982, 29–38; George L. Kelling and William J. Bratton, "Taking Back the Streets," *City Journal* 4, no. 3 (Summer 1994): 38–46.

15. Catherine M. Coles and George L. Kelling, "Prevention through Community Prosecution," *The Public Interest,* no. 136 (Summer 1999): 69–84.

16. John Seabrook, "Don't Shoot," *New Yorker,* June 22, 2009, 32–41; Christopher Winship and Jenny Berrien, "Boston Cops and Black Churches," *The Public Interest,* no. 136 (Summer 1999): 52–68; Jeffrey Rosen, "Prisoners of Parole," *New York Times Magazine,* January 10, 2010, 38–39.

17. Fox Butterfield, "Killing of Girl, 10, and Increase in Homicides Challenge Boston's Crime-Fighting Model," *New York Times,* July 14, 2002, 14.

18. David H. Bayley, "Learning about Crime—The Japanese Experience," *The Public Interest,* no. 44 (Summer 1976): 55–68; James Q. Wilson, "Crime and American Culture," *The Public Interest,* no. 70 (Winter 1983): 22–48.

19. Travis, *But They All Come Back,* chap. 12; Amy L. Solomon, Jenny Osborne, Laura Winterfield, Brian Elderbroom, Peggy Burke, Richard P. Stroker, Edward E. Rhine, and William D. Burrell, *Putting Public Safety First: 13 Parole Supervision Strategies to Enhance Reentry Outcomes* (Washington, DC: Urban Institute, December 2, 2008).

20. Petersilia, "When Prisoners Return to the Community"; Peggy B. Burke, "Collaboration for Successful Prisoner Reentry: The Role of Parole and the Courts," *Corrections Management Quarterly* 5, no. 3 (June 2001): 11–22.

21. Travis, *But They All Come Back,* chap. 13; Jeremy Travis, "But They All Come Back: Rethinking Prisoner Reentry," *Corrections Management Quarterly* 5, no. 3 (June 2001): 23–33.

22. The following discussion relies on Travis, *But They All Come Back,* chap. 7; Christopher Uggen and Jeremy Staff, "Work as a Turning Point for Criminal Offenders," *Corrections Management Quarterly* 5, no. 4 (September 2001): 1–16; and Dan Bloom, *Employment-Focused Programs for Ex-Prisoners: What Have We Learned, What Are We Learning, and Where Should We Go from Here?* (New York: MDRC, July 2006).

23. Manpower Demonstration Research Corporation, *Summary and Findings of the National Supported Work Demonstration* (Cambridge, MA: Ballinger, 1980), chap. 7.

24. Petersilia, *When Prisoners Come Home,* 99; Christopher Uggen, "Work as a Turning Point in the Life Course of Criminals: A Duration Model of Age, Employment, and Recidivism," *American Sociological Review* 65, no. 4 (August 2000): 529–46; Uggen and Staff, "Work as a Turning Point."

25. Sabol, West, and Cooper, "Prisoners in 2008," appendix table 11.

26. *Project RIO Strategic Plan, Fiscal Years 2008–2009* (Austin: Texas Department of Criminal Justice, Texas Workforce Commission, and Texas Youth Commission, March 2008).

27. Peter Finn, *Texas' Project RIO (Re-Integration of Offenders)* (Washington, DC: National Institute of Justice, June 1998).

28. Erin Jacobs and Bruce Western, *Report on the Evaluation of the ComALERT Prisoner Reentry Program* (New York: Office of the Kings County District Attorney, October 2007), chap. 3.

29. William B. Eimicke and Steven Cohen, "America Works' Criminal Justice Program: Providing Second Chances through Work" (New York: Manhattan Institute, November 2002).

30. The material that follows is based on interviews with CEO executive director Mindy Tarlow in 2006 and 2008; program materials; and Center for Employment Opportunities and MDRC, *The Power of Work: The Center for Employment Opportunities Comprehensive Prisoner Reentry Program* (New York: Center for Employment Opportunities, March 2006).

31. Sabol, West, and Cooper, "Prisoners in 2008," appendix table 11.

32. Erik Eckholm, "Experiment Will Test the Effectiveness of Post-Prison Employment Programs," *New York Times,* October 1, 2006, 18. The Joyce sites are in Chicago, Detroit, Milwaukee, and St. Paul. The evaluation is by MDRC.

33. Unless otherwise specified, the following information is based on materials downloaded from the web sites of the programs or their evaluators. On the Serious and Violent Offenders Reentry Initiative, I also relied on Alexander J. Cowell and Pamela K. Lattimore, "Impact of Prisoner Reentry Programming: Findings from the SVORI Multi-site Evaluation," presentation at the conference of the Association for Public Policy Analysis and Management (Research Triangle Park, NC, RTI International, November 7, 2008).

34. Christine Lundquist, Susan Brumbaugh, and Laura Winterfield, *Enrollment Issues among SVORI Programs* (Research Triangle Park, NC: RTI International, April 2006).

35. The information presented here is based on Dan Bloom, Cindy Redcross, Janine Zweig, and Gilda Azurdia, *Transitional Jobs for Ex-Prisoners: Early Impacts from a Random Assignment Evaluation of the Center for Employment Opportunities (CEO) Prisoner Reentry Program* (New York: MDRC, November 2007); and Cindy Redcross, "Transitional Jobs for Ex-Prisoners: Three-Year Results from a Random Assignment Evaluation of the Center for Employment Opportunities (CEO)," presented at the conference of the Association for Public Policy Analysis and Management, Boston, MA, November 4, 2010).

36. Interview and information from Mindy Tarlow, executive director of CEO, August 17 and September 15, 2008.

37. Cindy Redcross, Dan Bloom, Erin Jacobs, Michelle Manno, Sara Muller-Ravett, Kristin Seefeldt, Jennifer Yahner, Alford A. Young Jr., and Janine Zweig, *Work after Prison: One-Year Findings from the Transitional Jobs Reentry Demonstration* (New York: MDRC, October 2010); and private communication from Cindy Redcross, October 29, 2010. TJRD's one impact on recidivism was a 7 percent reduction in days spent in prison.

38. Finn, *Texas' Project RIO*. Finn summarizes the Texas A&M evaluation, which I was unable to obtain.

39. Jacobs and Western, "Report on the Evaluation of the ComALERT Prisoner Reentry Program," chaps. 5–8.

40. Chelsea Farley and Wendy S. McClanahan, "Ready4Work in Brief" (Philadelphia: Public/Private Ventures, May 6, 2007).

41. Pamela K. Lattimore and Christy Visher, "Assessment of the Serious and Violent Offender Reentry Initiative," testimony before the Appropriations Subcommittee on Commerce, Justice, Science and Related Agencies, U.S. Congress, March 13, 2009.

Chapter 5: Implementing Programs

1. Lawrence M. Mead, "Research and Welfare Reform," *Review of Policy Research* 22, no. 3 (May 2005): 401–21; Lawrence M. Mead, "Policy Research: The Field Dimension," *Policy Studies Journal* 33, no. 4 (November 2005): 535–57.

2. Studies of twenty-three states were conducted by the Urban Institute and the Rockefeller Institute of Government.

3. Lawrence M. Mead, *Government Matters: Welfare Reform in Wisconsin* (Princeton, NJ: Princeton University Press, 2004), chap. 11; Lawrence M. Mead, "State Political Culture and Welfare Reform," *Policy Studies Journal* 32, no. 2 (May 2004): 271–96.

4. See Dan Bloom and Kay Sherwood, *Matching Opportunities to Obligations: Lessons for Child Support Reform from the Parents' Fair Share Pilot Phase* (New York: Manpower Demonstration Research Corporation, April 1994). This study is outstanding. See also Fred Doolittle, Virginia Knox, Cynthia Miller, and Sharon Rowser, *Building Opportunities, Enforcing Obligations: Implementation and Interim Impacts of Parents' Fair Share* (New York: Manpower Demonstration Research Corporation, December 1998).

5. Karin Martinson, John Trutko, Demetra Smith Nightingale, Pamela A. Holcomb, and Burt S. Barnow, *The Implementation of the Partners for Fragile Families Demonstration Projects* (Washington, DC: Urban Institute, June 2007); Karin Martinson, John Trutko, and Debra Strong, "Serving Noncustodial Parents: A Descriptive Study of Welfare-to-Work Programs" (Washington, DC: Urban Institute, December 2000); Jessica Pearson, Nancy Thoennes, David Price, and Jane Venohr, *OCSE Responsible Fatherhood Programs: Early Implementation Lessons* (Denver: Center for Policy Research and Policy Studies, June 2000); Bernardine H. Watson, *Young Unwed Fathers Pilot Project: Initial Implementation Report* (Philadelphia: Public/Private Ventures, 1992).

6. Mark A. R. Kleiman, *When Brute Force Fails: How to Have Less Crime and Less Punishment* (Princeton, NJ: Princeton University Press, 2009).

7. Rebecca A. Maynard, "Paternalism, Teenage Pregnancy Prevention, and Teenage Parent Services," in *The New Paternalism: Supervisory Approaches to Poverty*, ed. Lawrence M. Mead (Washington, DC: Brookings, 1997), chap. 3.

8. Thomas Brock, David Butler, and David Long, *Unpaid Work Experience for Welfare Recipients: Findings and Lessons from MDRC Research* (New York: Manpower Demonstration Research Corporation, September 1993), chap. 3.

9. This was the consensus at a conference I organized titled "Why Did Welfare Caseloads Collapse? The Mystery of Diversion," held at the American Enterprise Institute, Washington, DC, November 14, 2008.

10. Judith M. Gueron and Edward Pauly, *From Welfare to Work* (New York: Russell Sage Foundation, 1991).

11. Erwin C. Hargrove, *The Missing Link: The Study of the Implementation of Social Policy* (Washington, DC: Urban Institute, 1975); David Brian Robertson, "Planned Incapacity to Succeed? Policy-Making Structures and Policy Failure," *Policy Studies Review* 8, no. 2 (Winter 1989): 241–63.

12. Michael Hill and Peter Hupe, *Implementing Public Policy: Governance in Theory and Practice* (London: Sage, 2002).

13. The classic statements of these two viewpoints appear in Jeffrey L. Pressman and Aaron Wildavsky, *Implementation*, 3rd ed. (Berkeley: University of California Press, 1984), and in Daniel A. Mazmanian and Paul A. Sabatier, *Implementation and Public Policy* (Glenview, IL: Scott, Foresman, 1983).

14. Lawrence M. Mead, "Welfare Reform in Wisconsin: The Local Role," *Administration and Society* 33, no. 5 (November 2001): 523–54.

15. Paul A. Sabatier, "Top-Down and Bottom-Up Approaches to Implementation Research: A Critical Analysis and Suggested Synthesis," *Journal of Public Policy* 6, no. 1 (January–March 1986): 21–48; Richard E. Matland, "Synthesizing the Implementation Literature: The Ambiguity-Conflict Model of Policy Implementation," *Journal of Public Administration Research and Theory* 5, no. 2 (April 1995): 145–74.

16. Ronald B. Mincy and Hillard Pouncy, "Paternalism, Child Support Enforcement, and Fragile Families," in *New Paternalism*, ed. Mead, 132–35.

17. Bloom and Sherwood, *Matching Opportunities to Obligations*, 17, 122–25.

18. Pearson et al., *Responsible Fatherhood Programs*, 99.

19. Bloom and Sherwood, *Matching Opportunities with Obligations*, 192.

20. Mead, *Government Matters*, 64–66, 230–31.

21. U.S. Congress, House Committee on Ways and Means, *2008 Green Book: Background Material, and Data on the Programs within the Jurisdiction of the Committee on Ways and Means* (Washington, DC: U.S. Government Printing Office, 2008), 8.77.

22. Jeremy Travis, *But They All Come Back: Facing the Challenges of Prison Reentry* (Washington, DC: Urban Institute Press, 2005), 59–60, 249–77, 350–51.

23. Doolittle et al., *Building Opportunities, Enforcing Obligations*, chap. 2; Bloom and Sherwood, *Matching Opportunities to Obligations*.

Chapter 6: The State Survey

1. This chapter is based largely on the work of Jon Flugstad, my research assistant at the American Enterprise Institute. He performed the state survey for the states other than the six I visited.

Chapter 7: Field Interviews

1. Daniel J. Elazar, *American Federalism: A View from the States,* 3rd ed. (New York: Harper and Row, 1984), chap. 5. Elazar calls these three cultures moralistic, individualistic, and traditionalistic.

2. Monica Davey, "Safety Is Issue as Budget Cuts Free Prisoners," *New York Times,* March 3, 2010, A1, A3.

3. For application of these factors to the implementation of TANF, see Lawrence M. Mead, *Government Matters: Welfare Reform in Wisconsin* (Princeton, NJ: Princeton University Press, 2004), 223–32; and Lawrence M. Mead, "State Political Culture and Welfare Reform," *Policy Studies Journal* 32, no. 2 (May 2004): 271–96.

4. Jyl J. Josephson, *Gender, Families, and State: Child Support Policy in the United States* (Lanham, MD: Rowman and Littlefield, 1997), 64–67, 74–76.

5. Department of Rehabilitation and Corrections, Ohio Department of Job and Family Services, Office of Child Support, and the Ohio CSEA Directors Association, *A Collaboration: Recommendations Report* (Columbus, OH: Department of Job and Family Services, January 2009).

6. Peter Finn, *Texas' Project RIO (Re-Integration of Offenders)* (Washington, DC: National Institute of Justice, June 1998), 11–12.

7. Mead, *Government Matters,* chaps. 5, 11–12.

Chapter 8: Recommendations

1. Thomas Brock, Fred Doolittle, Veronica Fellerath, and Michael Wiseman, *Creating New Hope: Implementation of a Program to Reduce Poverty and Reform Welfare* (New York: Manpower Demonstration Research Corporation, October 1997), chap. 5.

2. Jessica Pearson, Nancy Thoennes, David Price, and Jane Venohr, *OCSE Responsible Fatherhood Programs: Early Implementation Lessons* (Denver: Center for Policy Research and Policy Studies, June 2000), 80–84.

3. Mark Kleiman, "Coerced Abstinence: A Neopaternalist Drug Policy Initiative," in *The New Paternalism: Supervisory Approaches to Poverty,* ed. Lawrence M. Mead (Washington, DC: Brookings, 1997), chap. 6.

4. Joan Petersilia, *When Prisoners Come Home: Parole and Prisoner Reentry* (Oxford: Oxford University Press, 2003), chap. 5; Anne Morrison Piehl, *Preparing Prisoners for Employment: The Power of Small Rewards* (New York: Manhattan Institute, May 2009).

5. Dan Bloom and Kay Sherwood, *Matching Opportunities to Obligations: Lessons for Child Support Reform from the Parents' Fair Share Pilot Phase* (New York: Manpower Demonstration Research Corporation, April 1994), 192–93.

6. Ibid., chap. 7.

7. Robert I. Lerman, "Are Skills the Problem?" in *A Future of Good Jobs? America's Challenge in the Global Economy,* ed. Timothy J. Bartik and Susan N. Houseman (Kalamazoo, MI: Upjohn, 2008), chap. 2.

8. Susan Scrivener, Gayle Hamilton, Mary Farrell, Stephen Freedman, Daniel Friedlander, Marisa Mitchell, Jodi Nudelman, and Christine Schwartz, *National Evaluation of Welfare-to-Work Strategies: Implementation, Participation Patterns, Costs, and Two-Year Impacts of the Portland (Oregon) Welfare-to-Work Program* (Washington, DC: U.S. Department of Health and Human Services and U.S. Department of Education, May 1998).

9. In New York City, the welfare department lacked a sufficient capacity to place in the private sector, so it placed up to thirty-five thousand AFDC mothers in jobs in city departments in what was called the Work Experience Program. Wisconsin sought to enforce work immediately on one's application for welfare, so it had to guarantee community service positions for the least skilled.

10. Harry J. Holzer, Steven Raphael, and Michael A. Stoll, "How Do Employer Perceptions of Crime and Incarceration Affect the Employment Prospects of Less-Educated Young Black Men?" in *Black Males Left Behind,* ed. Ronald B. Mincy (Washington, DC: Urban Institute Press, 2006), chap. 3.

11. Christopher Jencks, *Rethinking Social Policy: Race, Poverty, and the Underclass* (Cambridge, MA: Harvard University Press, 1992), 127–28.

12. Peter Finn, *Texas' Project RIO (Re-Integration of Offenders)* (Washington, DC: National Institute of Justice, June 1998), 10.

13. Jeremy Travis, *But They All Come Back: Facing the Challenges of Prison Reentry* (Washington, DC: Urban Institute Press, 2005), 172–82; Bruce Western, "From Prison to Work: A Proposal for a National Prisoner Reentry Program" (Washington, DC: Brookings, December 2008).

14. Thomas Brock, David Butler, and David Long, *Unpaid Work Experience for Welfare Recipients: Findings and Lessons from MDRC Research* (New York: Manpower Demonstration Research Corporation, September 1993), table A.1.

15. Douglas J. Besharov and Peter Germanis, "Epilogue: Calculating WEP's Costs and Monetary Benefits," in *Managing Welfare Reform in New York City,* ed. E. S. Savas (Lanham, MD: Rowman and Littlefield, 2005), 210–22.

16. Manpower Demonstration Research Corporation, *Summary and Findings of the National Supported Work Demonstration* (Cambridge, MA: Ballinger, 1980), 146–48.

17. Cost figures were provided by America Works and the Center for Employment Opportunities.

18. America Works is paid $1,500 for jobs lasting at least 30 days, another $1,500 for jobs lasting 90 days, and $1,250 for jobs lasting at least 180 days. Clients served achieve these milestones at rates of about 75, 65, and 55 percent, respectively. Applying those percentages and charges to 1.3 million cases yields $3.4 billion in costs.

19. Western, "From Prison to Work," 23–24. Western's estimates are based on serving an incoming flow of 184,000 new parolees annually. Mine are based on serving a stock of parolees, new and old, with work problems, estimated at 492,706.

20. Brock, Butler, and Long, "Unpaid Work Experience," 55–59; Besharov and Germanis, "Epilogue."

21. Cynthia Miller and Virginia Knox, *The Challenge of Helping Low-Income Fathers Support Their Children: Final Lessons from Parents' Fair Share* (New York: Manpower Demonstration Research Corporation, November 2001), 26–27.

22. Manpower Demonstration Research Corporation, *National Supported Work Demonstration,* 146–48.

23. Western, "From Prison to Work," 24. Western's proposed program would cost $8,446 million. Against this estimate, he calculates offsets of $2,460 million from the value of the work produced by transitional employees, $250 million in increased earning capacity by the parolees, $4,010 from reduction in crime, and $4,050 from reductions in parole revocations—a total of $10,770 million.

24. James J. Stephan, "State Prison Expenditures, 2001," U.S. Department of Justice, Bureau of Justice Statistics, June 2004, table 2, yields a figure of $22,650 for 2001. I inflated this to $27,536 for 2008 using the national CPI for all urban consumers.

25. Hugh B. Price, "Transitioning Ex-Offenders into Jobs and Society," *Washingtonpost.com,* April 10, 2006.

26. Finn, *Texas' Project RIO,* 14–15; Chelsea Farley and Wendy S. McClanahan, "Ready4Work in Brief" (Philadelphia: Public/Private Ventures, May 6, 2007), 3–4.

27. Piehl, "Preparing Prisoners for Employment," 11–13.

28. Travis, *But They All Come Back,* 311–12.

29. Interview with Martin Horn, commissioner of Correction and Probation, New York City, November 26, 2008.

30. Brock, Butler, and Long, "Unpaid Work Experience," 17; Manpower Demonstration Research Corporation, *National Supported Work Demonstration,* 23, 35.

31. Michael Tonry and Mary Lynch, "Intermediate Sanctions," *Crime and Justice* 20 (1996): 99–144.

32. Christina Maslach, "Burned-out," *Human Relations* 5, no. 9 (September 1976): 16–22.

33. Bloom and Sherwood, *Matching Opportunities to Obligations,* chaps. 5, 7.

34. Austin Nichols and Elaine Sorensen, *The Impact of the New York EITC for Noncustodial Parents on Child Support Payments* (Washington, DC: Urban Institute, October 15, 2009).

35. Irwin Garfinkel, *Assuring Child Support: An Extension of Social Security* (New York: Russell Sage Foundation, 1992).

36. Internal Revenue Service web page (accessed November 11, 2010).

37. Peter Edelman, Harry J. Holzer, and Paul Offner, *Reconnecting Disadvantaged Young Men* (Washington, DC: Urban Institute Press, 2006), chap. 5; Wendell Primus, "Improving Public Policies to Increase the Income and Employment of Low-Income Nonresident Fathers," in *Black Males Left Behind,* ed. Mincy, chap. 9; Gordon L. Berlin, "Rewarding the Work of Individuals: A Counterintuitive Approach to Reducing Poverty and Strengthening Families," in *The Future of Children* 17, no. 2 (Fall 2007): 17–42.

38. Lawrence M. Mead, "The Twilight of Liberal Welfare Reform," *The Public Interest,* no. 139 (Spring 2000): 22–34.

39. David R. Riemer, "Replacing Welfare with Work: The Case for an Employment Maintenance Model," *Focus* 16, no. 2 (Winter 1994–1995): 23–30. Riemer's scheme, however, involves no requirement to work.

40. Bloom and Sherwood, *Matching Opportunities with Obligations,* 93–94, 194–95,

Chapter 9: National Policy

1. This discussion and the cost estimates are based on interviews with researchers at MDRC and officials at America Works and the U.S. Administration for Children and Families.

Index

Job availability, 15–16, 23, 82–83
  See also Guaranteed jobs programs
Job Corps, 28
Job losses in industry, 84, 85
Job retention issues, 57–58, 62, 64, 100
Job search/placement programs, 42
  See also Guaranteed jobs programs;
    Work programs
Job Service (federal), 74
Job Training Partnership Act, 27
Jobs Plus project, 25
Joint program opportunities, 106–7
Joyce Foundation, 59
Judges' roles, 73, 76, 92
Julia Carson Responsible Fatherhood
    and Healthy Families Act, 223
Justice, Department of, 60

Labor, Department of, 44, 60
Labor force participation, *See* Employ-
    ment participation rates
Lack of direction among poor men, 40
Low-skilled employment rates, 10, 15

Maintenance-of-effort (MOE) spending,
    112
Male psychology and nonwork
  accomplishment and competition,
    21–22, 101, 109–10
  assertiveness issues, 18–19, 29–30,
    31–32
  respect, drive for, 19–20, 23, 31
Mandatory *vs.* voluntary participation,
    29, 67, 96–97
  See also Incentives *vs.* requirements
Manhattan Institute, 85
Manpower Demonstration Research
    Corporation (MDRC), 42, 114–15
Marriage, 21, 33, 112
Mediation services, family relations, 42,
    47
Mexico, immigration from, 15–16

Michigan, 84, 88, 91
Michigan Prison Reentry Initiative
    (MPRI), 84, 88
Military model, 29–31
Minimum wage levels, 24
Mismatch theory, 16
Moynihan, Daniel Patrick, 22, 29
"Moynihan Report," 10–11

National Evaluation of Welfare-to-Work
    Strategies (NEWWS), 115
National Guard, 30
National Institute of Justice, 60
National policy perspective, future
  benefits recommendations, 116
  evaluation, 114–15
  funding, 111–14
  need for consensus, 116–17
  overview, 111
National Supported Work Demonstra-
    tion, 57, 102, 103, 105
Native American employment rates, 8–9
Native-born blacks, unique issues for,
    15–16
New Hope project, 25, 97
New Jersey, 84–85, 89, 92
New York
  field interview profile, 84–85, 89, 92
  projects in, 57–58, 58–59
Newark Prisoner Reentry Initiative, 85,
    93
No Child Left Behind Act, 26
Non-Custodial Parent (NCP) Choices
    program, 41–42, 47–48, 86, 88,
    91, 98
Nonpayer convictions, 86

Obama, Barack, 112
Obligation *vs.* opportunity, 5–6, 27–31,
    31–32, 39, 108
Office of Child Support Enforcement
    (OCSE), 36–37

About the Author

Lawrence M. Mead is professor of politics and public policy at New York University, where he teaches public policy and American government. He has been a visiting professor at Harvard, Princeton, and the University of Wisconsin. He has also been a visiting fellow at Princeton and at the Hoover Institution at Stanford.

Mr. Mead is an expert on the problems of poverty and welfare in the United States. Among academics, he was the principal exponent of work requirements in welfare, the approach that now dominates national policy. He is also a leading scholar of the politics and implementation of welfare reform programs. He has written seven books and over a hundred other publications on these subjects. These works have helped shape welfare reform in the United States and abroad.

Government Matters (Princeton University Press, 2005), Mr. Mead's study of welfare reform in Wisconsin, was a cowinner of the 2005 Louis Brownlow Book Award, given by the National Academy of Public Administration. More recently, he has also written and lectured on the sources of American primacy in the world.

Mr. Mead has consulted with federal, state, and local governments in the United States and with several foreign countries. He testifies regularly to Congress on poverty, welfare, and social policy, and he often comments on these subjects in the media.

He is a native of Huntington, New York, and a graduate of Amherst College. He received his Ph.D. in political science from Harvard University.